From Stumbling Blocks
to Stepping Stones

From Stumbling Blocks to Stepping Stones

The Life Experiences of Fifty Professional African American Women

Kathleen F. Slevin and
C. Ray Wingrove

NEW YORK UNIVERSITY PRESS
New York and London

NEW YORK UNIVERSITY PRESS
New York and London

Library of Congress Cataloging-in-Publication Data
Slevin, Kathleen F., 1947–
From stumbling blocks to stepping stones : the life experiences
of fifty professional African American women / Kathleen F. Slevin
and C. Ray Wingrove.
p.   cm.
Includes bibliographical references and index.
ISBN 0-8147-8099-7 (clothbound : alk. paper)
ISBN 0-8147-8100-4 (pbk. : alk. paper)
1. Afro-American women in the professions—Interviews.
2. Afro-American women—Social conditions. 3. Afro-American
women—Race identity. I. Wingrove, C. Ray, 1937–   II. Title.
E185.86.S63   1998
305.48'896073—ddc21   98-9091
                                                          CIP

New York University Press books are printed on acid-free paper,
and their binding materials are chosen for strength and durability.

Manufactured in the United States of America

10 9 8 7 6 5 4 3 2 1

Contents

Acknowledgments   *vii*

Introduction   1

1   Survival and Resistance: Early Lessons
    in the Family   11
    The Centrality of Racial Identity   11
    Learning to Survive and Resist   13

2   Survival and Resistance: Lessons
    in the Community   33
    The Black Community Remembered   34

3   The Church: Sacred and Secular Entwined   49
    Links among Church, Family, and Community   50
    The Centrality of the Church   52
    Social Life of Youth in the Church   54
    More Blending of the Sacred and the Secular   55
    The Church as a Shaper   56
    Teaching Gender Scripts and Racial Protest   59
    Gender and Class Tensions   61

4   Education: Passport to a Better Life   65
    Parents and Surrogates as Motivators   67
    Other Sources of Motivation   73
    Instilling Pride in Self and Race   75
    Black Schools and Black Teachers Remembered   79
    Limitations: The Impact of Race, Class,
        and Gender   84

5   The World of Work: Making It the Hard Way   87

    Limited Choices   88
    Working in an African American Environment
       during Legal Segregation   90
    Educators Doing Race and Gender Work   91
    Gender Matters in African American
       Work Settings   97
    Working with Whites during Legal Segregation   102
    Integration and the Elusiveness of Equality   108
    The Continuing Significance of Race
       and Gender   115
    Fighting Back   118

6   Free at Last: Surviving and Thriving
    in Retirement   123

    Free at Last   124
    Satisfaction with Retirement   125
    Old Wounds Revisited   147

7   Pioneer Role Models   151

    Lessons from the Past   153
    Lessons from the Present   156

    Appendix: Researchers' Comments
    on the Study   161

    Background   161
    Concerns of Race and Gender   162
    Interviews   163
    Creating a Collective Biography   165
    The Issue of Social Class   167
    An Overarching Theme   168
    The Authors   169

    Notes   171
    Index   181
    About the Authors   187

Acknowledgments

We are very fortunate to have a number of colleagues, students, and friends who were interested in and supportive of this project and of us. Our first debt of gratitude, however, is to the women whose life stories are the foundation of this book. Their willingness to talk to us, to share intimate details of their lives, and to complete our questionnaire makes this book possible. Several also took the time to read drafts of the manuscript and to offer suggestions for improvement. For all of their support we are deeply appreciative. We hope that our efforts reflect the respect and admiration in which we hold them.

Among our colleagues who gave generously of their time and talents, Toni Calasanti deserves special mention. From the earliest stages of the project, Toni offered constant support and encouragement. She helped us enormously as we struggled to conceptualize issues and to make sense of our data. She read endless drafts and provided insightful critiques. At a later stage, she was joined by Margaret Andersen, whose considerable editorial talents proved invaluable and led also to substantive revisions.

The generosity of other colleagues deserves mention, too. In a variety of ways, all helped to make this book possible, but we, of course, hold none accountable for any shortcomings of its content. Some provided critical contacts, and many read drafts of the manuscript and provided detailed commentary. All encouraged us to pursue this project because they believed in its importance. We list them alphabetically: David Aday, Lois Benjamin, John Sibley Butler, Gill Cell, Willie Dell, Fredi Epps-Jackson, Joe Feagin, Larry Griffin, Monica Griffin, Cindy

Hahamovich, Joy Haralick, Satoshi Ito, Clara Keith, Evans Kilker, Gary Kreps, Steve Kroll-Smith, Peg Miller, Gul Ozyegin, Evelyn Peevy, Ginny Powell, Ed Rhyne, Yana Rodgers, Miriam Rowe, Serbrenia Sims, Juanita Strawn, Carol Wharton, and Jeanne Zeidler.

Our students, both graduate and undergraduate, played important roles in helping us. Theresa Johnson spent an entire summer transcribing the tapes, and we thank her, not only for her excellent work but also for the cheerfulness and diligence with which she approached the task. Noir Fowler, Amy Vreeland, Amy Wollensack, and Erica McEachin-Rhodes read drafts and gave us valuable feedback, and we thank them for their contributions. Randy Russo provided valuable typing assistance, and we thank him. Our respective universities, The College of William and Mary and The University of Richmond (especially the Faculty Research Committee) provided varied assistance that enabled us to finish this book, and we thank them for their support.

All who have written books understand that the cost borne by the family members of the authors is considerable. Our story is no different. We want to thank our spouses, Bob Yeomans and Jane Wingrove, for their endless patience and support during the more than three years that it took to complete this project. We thank our children, Conor Slevin Yeomans, Sarah Slevin Yeomans, and Benjamin Wingrove, who were so constantly amazed that two people could take so long to complete one task.

Finally, we express great appreciation to our editor, Niko Pfund, for his wisdom, support, and good humor while seeing us through this project.

Introduction

I felt that everything that I attempted, I got hit on the head or kicked in the pants or just flat knocked down. And I've always strived to be the best because I knew that everybody was breathing down my throat because [I am] Black and female.   (State government senior management retiree)

I got my first speaking experience in the church. [In the church] you could develop leadership skills. People learned to trust you. You could take up the offering. . . . You learned a sense of self-confidence in the church.

(Retired social worker)

At that time the rule of thumb was [that] you had to come out of the classroom [without pay] before you wore maternity clothes. So, at the end of your third month you had to come out. And you couldn't come back until the child was eight months old.   (Retired elementary school teacher)

I have no regrets, and I think it's because I'm a versatile person. I have a lot of skills and talents. . . . I roll and bounce back with the punches. I don't tend to get upset easy, or to wallow in anything. I think about it, and do what I'm going to do about it and move on.   (Retired university professor)

Fifty retired professional African American women sat with us in their homes and shared these and countless other reminiscences from their past.[1] They spent hours talking about key aspects of their lives. They recalled childhood relationships with parents, siblings, neighbors, and teachers. They indicated their pleasures and displeasures related to both paid and unpaid work experiences. They described lives of achievement and success in the face of impediments arising from their race and gender. They spoke of overcoming obstacles that most people would consider overwhelming, and they remembered persisting when often they only wanted to quit. They learned to depend on their ingenuity and to turn adversity into motivation. As one woman aptly expressed it, "We made stepping stones from stumbling blocks."

We met and interviewed these women in the summer and fall of 1993 and the spring of 1994. Inclusion in the study required that a woman be African American and a retired professional career person. We began the process with the help of two associates, both prominent African American women who live in different cities in Virginia. They understood the nature of our study and identified women who met our criteria. One of these "informants" had a master's degree and had been a college professor, a community leader, and, finally, the director of a large urban day care center for the aged. The other was a retired college professor and administrator who had earned her doctorate from a prestigious northern university.

Armed with lists of women from our "informants," we sent a letter of introduction to each woman in which we identified ourselves as social science researchers. We gave the name of the woman who recommended her and described the nature of the study. We told the women that our pilot interviews had led us to believe that interviews would last two and a half to three hours and that a questionnaire would be left behind for them to complete, which would take twenty or thirty additional minutes of their time. We concluded our letters by asking that they consider granting us interviews and by telling them that we would telephone within a week, hoping to arrange an interview appointment.

Our initial telephone contacts were met with enthusiasm. (Only one woman refused an interview.) All interviews were conducted in the homes of the women. The interviews averaged three hours, but some lasted five hours. With the exception of three women who were uncomfortable being recorded, all interviews were taped. At the close of each interview, we asked for additional names of retired professional or business women who might agree to be interviewed. Using this snowball approach, we continued interviewing until our sample size reached fifty.

Generally, interviews were cordial and relaxed, and we often shared aspects of our lives with the women. The women were very open, forthright, and sometimes emotional. There was lots of laughter and, occasionally, tears. We were both struck by the level of frankness expressed and by the amount of intimate details about their lives the women were willing to reveal. Interviews were supplemented with information, gathered in questionnaires, about lifestyles, satisfactions, and social relationships in retirement.

Although at the time of interview the women ranged in age from fifty-three to eighty-seven, only three were in their fifties. Thirty-six women were aged sixty-five or over, and the average age was sixty-nine. Only one self-employed businesswoman in our group lacks any college experience. Twenty-four women hold master's degrees, and nine have earned doctorates. Their preretirement profile shows that eight retired as college professors, and twenty-eight had held a variety of teaching/supervisory positions in elementary or secondary education. The remaining fourteen represented careers in state or federal government, medicine, nursing, public service, and self-employment. Most of them had married, and twenty-five still live with their spouses. A majority of the seventeen widows and the six who are divorced or separated live alone, but seven of them share homes with a relative or companion.

The women we interviewed resided in Virginia and, with few exceptions, had spent most of their lives in the South. Their lives, however, illuminate experiences that teach us to look beyond regional identity. We do not minimize the impact of geographical location on life experiences, but we also believe that, because these women lived most of their lives when segregation was pervasive throughout the United States (de jure in the South and de facto in the North), the salience of geographical location is attenuated. In addition, the issues that we examine in looking at their lives are less likely than others to be affected in major ways by differing geographical locations.

The stories these fifty women told transported us to the earlier decades of this century as they related how they came of age during the era of legal segregation. They told us what it was like to be educated and to work in both segregated and integrated worlds. They shared with us what it was like to retire from the world of paid employment, and they spoke of their joys and concerns in dealing with advancing years and what they liked and disliked about being older women. It became apparent that they are role models and sources of inspiration for women of *all* races. The ways in which they navigated challenges and continue to live active and productive lives can be instructive for *all* people. In fact, these Black women personified independence, strength, and a "can do" approach to life long before these traits were legitimized for White women by the women's movement.

These women are *pioneers*, and, as such, they are models for young women of today who are just beginning the journey they have completed. Their life stories provide insights into the multiple dilemmas and obstacles that women face in various settings. Through them we come to appreciate the complexities of their lives and the ways in which they asserted themselves in the face of adversity. The importance of their life stories to younger generations is illustrated by the following comments written by a twenty-year-old African American college woman just after she had read a rough draft of this book. She wrote:

> Reading about the lives of the Black women before me was a rewarding experience. Although I had heard about the way in which

African American women of their generation had been treated, hearing their stories personalized it for me and helped me to really comprehend their struggles. I am grateful for what these women have done for the members of my generation. Their hard work and motivation to succeed paved the way for me to be here in college. . . . I was struck by the universality of these women's overriding message. Black or White, male or female, community ties—through neighborhoods, churches, schools, and work places—are important. Education is important; a strong work ethic is important. It is not only Black women who can benefit from the lessons exhibited in these women's lives. It is important that members of my generation follow these examples of mentoring and volunteering to continue the progress that these amazing women have made. As Black women today move ahead, we need to reach back to those who fill the positions that we have vacated and help them. The result of this cycle of mentoring will benefit Black women nationwide and help complete the work that those fifty retirees began—a work towards equality for African American women, and, in truth, all women in all areas of life. Their lives and efforts are commendable. My generation of Black women owe them our gratitude and respect.

We believe that the experiences of these women in retirement can also serve as a model for today's middle-aged women who will be retiring in the first part of the twenty-first century. Beginning in 2010, millions of baby boomers (most of whom will be women) will begin to swell the ranks of aged Americans. They will continue in the avalanche until 2030. Unlike past generations, the millions of women who will be reaching their old age between 2010 and 2030 are likely to have spent their adult lives in the paid labor force. They are more likely than women of the past to have pensions, social security, and savings in their own names. They are more likely to have completed high school and college. They are more likely to have entered professions and to have followed discernable career paths. In short, they are more likely to be like the women in this study. Like them, they will face retirement after a lifetime of employment. Like them, more older women in the twenty-first century will have combined mothering and work roles and have developed coping strategies to meet the demands of family, work, and community. As well as providing a legacy of survival and resistance, these women point the way to creating a positive sense of self as older women in a society that devalues such women. Whatever their hurdles in younger life, whatever the challenges of growing old, these women lead lives that are graphic testimonies to successful aging. Thus, these women provide a rich legacy to future generations of women—Black and White—who will leave the workforce after a lifetime of continuous employment and who look for guidance in how to live productive and happy lives as they grow old.

The lives of these Black women also dispel the monolithic image of older African American women as being poor, uneducated, and sick inhabitants of blighted inner-city areas.[2] Their individual lives taken collectively demand—in a way that statistics cannot—that we acknowledge the diversity that exists among older Black women and that we recognize the richness, complexity, and depth of their experiences. They are living proof that at least some elderly Black American women are doing quite well financially and socially and that not all of them experience old age ravished by illness and disability. They enjoy active and rich lives in the retirement years, and they take satisfaction in the enhanced opportunities this stage of life allows for them to spend time with family and friends, to travel, and to be involved in church and community activities. They are living contradictions to the persistent myth cited by sociologist Jacquelyne Jackson that older Black American women are resistant to retirement because it is only in paid work that they can find status and meaning in their lives.[3] While their lives in no way detract from the realities of the harsh conditions in which many older Black American women live today, they do debunk the prevalent image that *all* old Black American women fit that description.

Despite their privilege, these retired professional African American women lead lives still tainted by oppression. It is precisely their status as privileged African American women that provides us the opportunity to illustrate—in a manner that could not be achieved by looking at the lives of poor women—the tensions between privilege and power, on the one hand, and the oppression caused by the interacting forces of racism and sexism, on the other. This same point is made by the African American anthropologist Irma McClaurin-Allen when she discusses the choice of elite Black American women as a useful focus of scholarly attention. She argues that "their life stories make visible the forces that constrain individual potential and ultimately structure the way black women may live their lives in a variety of circumstances. We come to see the subtle and conflicting ways social categories interact to create domains of privilege and of oppression."[4]

We were guided in our search for recurrent themes in these women's lives by the life course and feminist perspectives. A life course perspective is described by the sociologists Eleanor Stoller and Rose Gibson as one that explores "the ways in which people's social location, the historical period in which they live, and their personal biography shape their experience."[5] This perspective requires that we remain sensitive to how the time period in which people live relegates them to prescribed social roles, which in turn limit their opportunities and narrow their life chances. At the same time, of course, identical historical events can have very dissimilar meanings for different individuals' lives, depending on their social locations.

The life course perspective also points out the importance of cohort analysis in understanding the connection between human resources and historical events.[6] This component, however, we chose to ignore. As we examined our data, we recognized the extent to which the lives of the women in our sample defied such analysis. A pervasive similarity characterized so many of their descriptions of critical life experiences that the absence of cohort differences was often palpable. In a fundamental way, their lives were powerfully shaped by structural constraints that were ubiquitous and consistent. All grew up in a society characterized by segregation, and all received the bulk of their education in such a system. The effects of racism, intertwined with systems of class and gender inequality, created a pervasive and homogenous oppression for most of their lives and negated, we believe, the usefulness of cohort analysis.

The feminist perspective blends well with that of the life course as it insists that we consider the importance of race, social class, and gender and their intersections with the impact of historical events and individual biographies. We were also sensitive to the feminist refusal to use men's experiences as the pivotal standard for understanding the lives of women.

The first several chapters focus on the major institutions and critical life circumstances that shaped these women's lives. We explore their legacies—those given to them and those they pass on. As we examine their collective biographies within the context of the family, the school, the church, and the community, we are aware of the vast historical documentation of these institutions in the lives of Black segregated America. We do not attempt to replicate or even to summarize that body of literature. Rather, we try to show the historical importance of those institutions through the eyes of women who lived that history. We hear them tell the story in their own words, and, in that way, they make history come alive through their individual biographies.

Chapter 1 examines the early lessons that occurred within the family setting. We hear how the themes of survival and resistance surfaced early in childhood. As youngsters, they learned critical lessons in how to handle the challenges they would face as African Americans in U.S. society. Those messages, absorbed in the home, were reinforced and strengthened in the broader settings of community, church, and school—the topics covered respectively in chapters 2, 3, and 4. Chapter 5 deals with their employment experiences, and we listen to their accounts of struggles and triumphs in both segregated and integrated work environments. In chapter 6, we shift to their retirement from paid employment, which exemplifies a special kind of freedom to them. We view the close link between their past and their present, and we quickly realize that their comforts and contentments in retirement are not happenstance but rather a reflection of lifetimes of thoughtful planning and preparation. Finally, in chapter 7, we highlight what we see as the most compelling lessons from their life stories.

1

Survival and Resistance
Early Lessons in the Family

[My parents] were always teaching us to do whatever was right; to be honest. They were anxious that we would complete school as much as we could. They wanted us to be self-reliant and reliable.

> (Retired high school math teacher—the
> youngest child of four and the only girl)

Like most people, the women in our study saw their families in general, and their parents in particular, as the singularly most important influence in their formative years. Their families taught them how to deal with the inevitable adversities they would confront as African Americans in the United States. In this sense, their parents were crucial to their survival in a way not typical for White Americans. Some childhood lessons were so powerful in their impact that even now, in retirement, the women remember them vividly. Whatever the lesson—the need to be economically independent, to avoid hurtful Whites, to choose between battles, or literally to fight for survival—one cannot help but appreciate the power of these legacies of survival and resistance in their lives.

The Centrality of Racial Identity

The forces of race, gender, class, and age combine in various shifting and interdependent ways to frame the stage on which the young are raised. Despite the importance of their interdependence, however, the influence of one system may at times overshadow that of the others. Certainly, this is how these women explained the dominance of race in their early lives.[1] Being a Black American during that time meant that race was the pervasive and inescapable force that defined and dominated their experiences. It overshadowed all other identities. "You knew you were Black from the day you were born . . . everything was segregated," was how one woman remembered the importance of race and racial segregation in her childhood. Daily living was certainly constrained by gender and class hierarchies, but, in a profound sense, racial hierarchy was the overwhelming force that dominated the consciousness of Black Americans during these decades.[2] The life stories of the few women whose fathers' economic and social circumstances allowed for relatively affluent lifestyles affirm that the combination of social class privilege and maleness could not defy the power of racism even in rich Black men's lives.

Rearing children to understand and to live in two cultural milieus—one Black, one White—presents unique challenges to Black American parents in any time period. In a legally and rigidly segregated setting, however, Black parents had to be even more vigilant and creative in what and how they taught their children. They had to teach them to feel good about themselves and yet to deal with the inevitable contradictions that accompany being a member of an oppressed group formally defined as second-class citizens. These young Black American girls had to learn to appreciate the difference between what was ideal and what was reality. They had to learn to strive for as much education as possible, since education represented the only viable escape from a life of labor in the White man's kitchen. At the same time, they had to learn that, no matter how much education they achieved, their opportunities would still be limited by their race. Thus, the facts of life crucial to their survival had to encompass the inevitability of both institutional racism and personal discrimination. Indeed, the inextricable tensions of race, gender, and class systems shaped a social construction of reality that, while first experienced in the context of early childhood, would be continuously revisited from childhood through old age.

It is thus not surprising that the theme of survival and resistance resonates throughout these women's early childhoods. Their reminiscences make clear that parents and surrogates found ways to teach them self-respect and racial pride even in the face of denigration and racial hatred. One retiree who grew up in poor circumstances recalled her parents' constant advice to "hold your head up. No matter how poor you are, you're as good as anyone else, regardless of color." Another, in describing her close-knit family, said, "We were encouraged to love each other, to protect each other, and to stand by each other."

Learning to think well of themselves and to be the best were integral lessons of their early years. Childhood lessons ran the gamut from the subtle to the obvious, and most reflected the lived experiences of mothers and fathers whose own family lives bore keen memories of slavery and oppression. From the example of their elders, these Black American youngsters learned that the lessons of childhood must form the basis of lifelong learning and that negotiating negative experiences and encounters— "turning negatives into positives," as more than one woman put it—must become, if not second nature, then a practiced art of survival in a hostile world.

Learning to Survive and Resist

Through the recollections of women now wise and seasoned from decades of exposure to oppression and practice in dealing with discrimination and racism, we hear firsthand how lived experience—both their own and that of others close to them—became a guiding force that shaped their responses to structures and events. Their childhood stories show how they navigated the many contradictions they faced and developed perspectives that allowed them some level of control over their lives. Equally important, they reveal how they developed positive self-identities as young Black American women, despite how they were viewed by members of the dominant White society.

"Avoid Hurtful Whites"

As part of their race work, parents and other adults had to protect young children from contact with Whites who might harm them. Most of these women recall how their parents, especially in early childhood, tried to shield them from the harshness of segregation and from racist encounters.[3] A typical comment was, "We were sheltered and protected from a lot of things." The majority who lived in the isolation of heavily segregated communities often had their direct exposure to racism delayed. Those few who grew up in patterns of living arrangements that brought them closer to Whites had constant reminders of racial hierarchy. The importance of physical boundaries is reflected in statements made by a couple of the women. One said, "I lived in a Black world. We did not have White neighbors. I did not have any associations." And another remembered, "I had not been around White people . . . was not around anybody but the nurturing good Black folk. . . . I was living in a Black world. I never thought about it. Just moving along, enjoying my growing and just developing that self-confidence— being nurtured." In this second quote, we also hear how the hindsight provided by age allows for a heightened level of insight.

Some women lived close enough to Whites to have White children as playmates. In such cases, specific incidents of racial bigotry quickly shattered their sense of childhood innocence. A retired school principal recalled an early and particularly hurtful experience. "I was more aware that I was Black, and it was because we . . . lived in such close proximity to Whites in our community. And I had, as a little girl, a friend who was White who went to a different school than I. And I remember the thing that hurt me most is [that] one day I was coming from school (I had to walk by her school to get home), and she was with some of her friends. And I spoke, and she did not speak to me. . . . I guess that's what really hurt." (This woman was one of the youngest we interviewed, which reinforces the notion that the days of legal segregation fostered a monotonous sameness of racial inequality, prejudice, and discrimination regardless of the decade in which these women grew up.) Another particularly poignant story told by a retired university administrator who grew up in comfortable circumstances in the Midwest illustrates the pain associated with early encounters with racism:

> You know when you start to school in the first grade, you're just a kid, right? You just accept everybody else. They accept you. And so, Mary Jane Sanke and I—she was a White girl, and they lived not too far from us, and we'd been playing together, hopscotch, and you know, skipping rope, things like that [that] girls play. Black jacks. Mary Jane had a birthday party. I was not invited. Mary Jane was upset, and so was I. But my mother explained to me what had happened—that Mary Jane's mother did not understand the relationship between the two of us. And Mary Jane's mother thought that I would be out of place at her party—the only Black child there.

In the long run, place of residence and proximity to Whites made little difference in the women's ultimate experiences with prejudice and discrimination in a racist world. Even those youngsters who lived in a separate Black world, with little personal experience of racial prejudice, spoke of their awareness of racial inequality, which came to them through the discussed experiences of others. A woman who grew up in considerable comfort on the outskirts of a sizable Southern town and whose father was employed in a well-paid, skilled job in a racially mixed setting said, "It was only through my dad that we would hear these comments [about racism and prejudice]. . . ." Still, parents tried to protect their young as long as possible and in as many ways as possible. Social class influenced the manner in which some parents tried to offer protection. The comments of a physician's daughter, for example, highlights the advantage of economic resources as an additional shield. She said, "I didn't run into a lot of that [separate facilities] because Daddy had a car by that time, and he was practicing [medicine], so we didn't have to go on the streetcar. We didn't have to do other things, and he took us where we went. And he did his best to make sure we weren't exposed to it [discrimination], if possible."

The memories of a university professor who grew up in considerable affluence illustrate, however, that class could not defy the ubiquity of racism and prejudice. African Americans were allowed to use the public parks in her city only one day out of the year. That day was in June, when Black Independence Day was celebrated. Of segregation, she said, "It was just a way of life. Being Black was . . . just the way you were. I became more aware of it after I left home. . . . The recognition of the end of slavery was sporadic throughout the South, and in Dover Town, we celebrated June 19. And we could go to all the parks and picnics [only] on that day."

Hence, we see why Black American parents understood the need to create what the African American anthropologist Irma McClaurin-Allen calls "an emotional sanctuary" as an essential part of self-protection in a world of racial hatred.[4] The ability to create boundaries, whether physical or emotional, to construct safe spaces that were largely restricted to other Black Americans, became something that influenced the lives of these women from early childhood on.

"Be the Best"

Like their parents before them, these women's parents dreamed of a better life for their children. Thus, the ideals of achievement and success so typical of the "American Dream" were an important message conveyed to the women as youngsters. Parental emphasis on excelling was a pervasive one in the stories told to us. Nevertheless, it was understood that Black Americans' successes would have to be realized within the confines of a segregated world. For them, "making it" could never be the same as for Whites. One woman's comment reflects this as she recalled the message her parents gave her: "Do your best whatever you're doing. If it's a garbage man or woman or whatever, be the best."

The demand to do their best went beyond verbal entreaty. Parents, and specifically mothers, who oversaw the running of the household, pushed their daughters. Whether the task at hand was a household chore or a homework assignment, the message was clear that shoddy work was unacceptable and that nothing but the best would pass muster. Indeed, several women specifically recalled being required to re-do a chore until they "got it right."

Excelling—doing one's very best—was recognized as essential in order to reach even minimal levels of success. The specific forms of racism extant in segregation forced Black Americans to use different strategies to fulfill the dream. These strategies reflected their lack of legal recourse in the face of unjust treatment by the White majority and the higher stakes that accompanied being Black. Thus, while the values learned by Black children— education, hard work, honesty, responsibility—appeared to mirror the values of White society, they were often distinctly racialized. In fact, they were frequently taught from a basis of resistance to the dominant society rather than as acquiescence to it. This point is illustrated in a story told by a retiree who had grown up in abject poverty in the rural South and whose parents worked for a local White farmer and his wife. On weekends and holidays, the girls in her family were required to work for the same family. She recollected angrily how deeply resentful all the members of her family felt toward this particular White couple because they so openly and consistently treated them with disrespect. Tearfully, she recounted her parents' instructions to her and her sister about how they should approach their Saturday house cleaning jobs:

They [parents] wanted to be sure that we understood our positions, and they would say to us, "Even if you have to dust around money, leave it laying there. I don't care if it's on the floor. Leave it laying there. Don't give them a chance to think that you'll take a dime." And I would dust around it because I didn't want them to even think that I attempted to move a penny or two pennies or three pennies or whatever. And, yet, it would be tempting. But you knew that you didn't do that because . . . you know, I'm going to be honest, what they thought, what we heard that all White folks thought about Black folks is—they stink and they steal. And, you know, our parents were so adamant about the fact that they didn't want us to be in that category.

This narrative suggests that these girls had to live up to standards that would have far exceeded those expected of White children. They had to exceed the norm in an attempt to combat racial stereotypes. They had to be better than the best.[5] It demonstrates also how some values, in this case honesty, were not just an emulation of the dominant culture but rather reactions and resistance to it.

"Keep Your Skirt Down and Your Pants Up"

Women remembered that parents were much more restrictive of girls' activities than they were of boys'. Parents saw daughters as presenting a special headache. They had an obsessive fear that their girls might become pregnant while young and unmarried. Pregnancy outside the confines of marriage would seriously hinder, if not kill, their daughters' chances of becoming achievers. Although this problem was not race-specific, there were circumstances surrounding it that were particularly racialized. Legal segregation of Black communities created housing patterns that made it difficult for Black parents to control the contacts their daughters had with neighborhood boys of different social classes. Thus, a kind of double jeopardy was created. Parents recognized that most young Black men in their communities were in economically precarious positions that made them unsuitable as early fathers or mates, a fact that stood in contrast to the situations of middle-class Whites. Consequently, African American parents perceived themselves as facing special challenges in managing the sexual encounters of their daughters. Although their issues were different, in this regard they paralleled the gender asymmetry of the dominant society.

Many women in our study recalled parental anxiety and suspicion about their whereabouts, especially after they reached puberty. They mentioned the special role fathers assumed in preaching sexual modesty and abstinence for girls in the family. It was not uncommon for parents across the spectrum of social classes to resort to chaperons or strict parental supervision of daughters when they were dating. A woman who grew up poor told what it was like in her family. As she remembered it, "We could dance, but since couples danced close then, we were not allowed to dance at night. Morning or breakfast dances were held in some nearby community building. Young people would go and parents would serve brunch type food, and we would dance. But we were chaperoned by adults even then." A woman from a more affluent home told a similar story:

> [Mother] knew what she had taught me. But Daddy was practicing medicine, and he saw lots of pregnant girls, and he was determined that I wasn't going to be one . . . and in the summer, my daddy would be certain that every month . . . we had a party at my house. And, we'd go on hayrides and that type of thing. But . . . you had a chaperon. I was seventeen years old and out of high school before I ever went to the movies alone with a fellow.

Another woman who grew up in a sizable Southern city and who was one of thirteen children remembered her father "walking behind her and her friends" when they left teenage social events. She laughed as she recalled how her father constantly preached, "Keep your dress down and your pants up." She went on to recount the effectiveness of her father's admonitions: "I got married a virgin and was scared to death on my wedding night!" Parents' strictness with their daughters is also evident in the remembrances of yet another woman, who said:

She [Mom] would believe anything my sister said. I would get whippings because of what my sister told about me on dates. For example, once I had a date with a big football player from the local college. We were in our living room and [were] sitting very close to the coal stove. He reached over and touched my leg and said, "You're going to burn your leg." My sister told my mother that he was feeling my leg. That boy was chased off, and I was never allowed to date him again.

"Pick Your Battles"

Regardless of how protected they might have been as young children, women told us how as children they soon learned the social meaning of race and some of the strategies to resist racism. When asked to identify some major turning points in her life, a retired federal employee said that it was when she first realized "as a small kid" that "Blacks couldn't go certain places or do certain things." Black parents had to teach general principles of resistance because in day-to-day life there was an endless array of unpredictable issues and encounters to face. The context of racism and oppression was constantly changing, so adaptability and creativity were critical tools of survival for all African Americans. The young had to learn how to see racism as external to them, to understand it as something beyond the individual—that it was systemic. At the same time, they had to handle racism and prejudice on a personal level. Even though they understood that *all* Black Americans were treated unequally, they also had to deal with the reality of what that inequality meant for them personally. In other words, they had to be ready to deal with the institutionalized constraints as well as the personal hatred and prejudice.

What were these women taught that helped them face these issues and allowed them to feel in control of their own lives? A key strategy was learning when to fight and when to avoid confrontation—something that became an important lifelong skill in navigating hostile situations. Parents and other adults taught these youngsters how to "pick their battles." Clearly, there was a time to fight, but there were also times when fighting openly was not the best option. If too much was at stake or if, as one woman put it, "they [Whites] had *all* the cards," then protecting one's interests was the pragmatic thing to do. This is illustrated in a story told by the woman who grew up in the Midwest:

> My brother was very popular in high school. And so, when he be-came a senior, the senior class wanted to run him for [the class] pres-idency. The principal called him in and told him, "Kenny, I under-stand that there's a move . . . on to elect you as president of the se-nior class. Well, I want to tell you right now that has never happened in this school, and it's not going to happen this year. So, if you want to graduate, you'd better back out right now." He did. So, my brother backed out. He wanted to graduate.

A retired university professor from an affluent background in a small southern town recalled another lesson that highlights the emphasis on choosing battles. Her parents taught her and her siblings to circumvent neighborhoods where they might come to harm. As youngsters, they were threatened by White children whose house they had to pass on their way downtown. She de-scribed how her parents taught them how to recognize the con-ditions under which hostility was likely to erupt and how to avoid confrontation:

> I can remember that we used to walk to town. And there was a fam-ily of White kids, I don't know how many, but I would say seven, eight, nine, or ten. And when Black kids would pass their house . . . [they would] push them off the sidewalk. So the answer to that was—don't go down that street. Go the other way . . . that's what the fam-ily taught us all . . . you don't go that street. Turn two blocks before you get there.

Although the two incidents cited are very different, the deci-sion to avoid confrontation was the same. By doing so, in each case the Black youngster preserved something of value. In both instances, nonresistance was the route to survival. Yet, by all accounts, values had to be weighed carefully lest nonresistance compromise integrity.

Sometimes, with a little creativity, a situation could be manipulated to one's advantage. The daughter of an upwardly mobile businessman referred to this as "strategizing." She explained how her father would do that by the way in which he chose his words when putting together a deal with a White man.

As she remembered:

> He [father] would talk about his business transactions and talk about how he would put over a sale or a transaction without ever being dishonest . . . maybe by answering the way the person wanted him to answer or something. Strategizing. That's the only thing I can think of, and I don't know if that's a good word to use. But I guess he taught that there's more than one way to accomplish your aim—your goal. But you don't ever give up your integrity.

Again, we see that, regardless of the strategy chosen, it was always important to maintain integrity. Sometimes passive resistance might be the route to self-respect and a feeling of integrity. Such was the case of the woman whose mother forbade her to patronize White restaurants that served Blacks through side windows. Her mother said, "'Don't you ever let me see you do that as long as you live. Don't ever go to a window to get any [food]' . . . because that was another way of putting you down. And she said, 'You don't do that.' So we did not . . . they kept us away from it. That is the way they protected us."

But sometimes resistance was bolder, and behavior bordered on outright defiance of the unwritten rules of apartheid. Freedoms permitted by Whites were tested and pushed to the limits as a way of expressing Black Americans' rights to equality. Testing the rules without risking undue harm required astute observation of subtle cues from mentors. The following scenario depicts such an occasion:

> The only thing that I can really put a hand on . . . is that we knew that these things existed, not that they [parents] were accepting of what the situation was. But you know, [at the time] you had to ride

in the back of the bus. So . . . when you get on the bus, go to the clos-
est seat that was to the middle of the bus . . . you don't necessarily
have to go deep into the back of the bus. . . . I guess my father used
to always preach that this was kind of unfair, which it was unfair.

Still, there were times when avoidance, strategizing, passive
resistance, and all the other nonviolent tactics were not enough.
There were times when the ugliness of racism came crashing
down on Blacks and demanded that risks be taken, to preserve
not only integrity but, indeed, life itself. There were times when
backs were against the wall, and there was no alternative but to
stand and fight. Such is the case in the following account, vividly
remembered by a woman who grew up in a small town in North
Carolina:

I was a little girl, about six, I'd say. And we lived, you know, how the
towns were divided. All the Black folk were across the railroad tracks.
And it was said in the town . . . some Black boy had been down on
the main street where the White high school was, standing across the
street looking at the White girls. Well, that evening they were going
around trying to find this boy. Fifty White men on horses with big
guns and things. So they came to our house, and my father went out
to meet them. He said, "Good evening, gentlemen." And they were
trampling all over my mother's flowers and prancing all around.

And they said they wanted him to bring my brother out—to take
his hat out, his coat out, his little jacket that he wore and everything,
to let them see because they had a description. And you know it, that
sort of impressed the girls, because he didn't act like he was scared or
nothing; he just told them to bring his coat and hat out; and my
Daddy went out there, and then my brother faced them. My mother!
We were shocked at her. She was loading shotguns. They loved to
hunt. We had plenty shotguns. And we were crying, and she said,
"Shut up that crying, because we are going to fight! If they get one of
us, they're going to get all." And honey, she was loading shotguns
and giving us positions, and she said, "All I ask you to do is to get
one." And I tell you and from that day forward . . . I've never been
afraid of White people ever again. You know I could always face any
confrontation that I had. Ah, but she said, "Oh, no, we are going to
fight!" Un, un, she said, "Today, if one goes, everybody goes."

So after they looked at him and looked at the jacket and the coat, they decided that he was not the one, and they went on. But boy, I tell you, when me and my sisters were in there, we were crying and wailing. She said, "Shut up! Stop that crying and you get by this window, and you get by that window, and here, Bessie [making motion of receiving a shotgun], and all you got to do is aim it and pull the trigger." Never had a gun in my hand in my life. I said, "Oh Lord, no." But she was a brave little woman. Yeah, she was really a tower.

Some battles were worth fighting. Some battles *had* to be fought. To do anything less would mean the denigration of personal honor and integrity. The words of the speaker's parents after that episode strengthened this message and remain with her to this day. "If you know you're not guilty, if you haven't done anything, don't back down off nobody. You know. Don't back down." And so, she said, "You know, we grew up being strong like that."

"You're as Good as Anybody Else"

Parents taught some forms of resistance that were more subtle and psychological than those already discussed. For example, they taught their daughters to view life with a positive attitude and to build inner strength and self-esteem. In other words, they taught them to develop an armor of resistance to negative messages. Time and time again, women alluded to this armor and how they learned to use it to their advantage. A woman whose family moved from the working to the middle class during her childhood remembered a painful lesson as she acquired her armor of resistance. She related a conversation she had with her mother just before she began elementary school in a Northern city:

"You're going to be called a nigger." "What's that?" "That's a derogatory name that people use for Negro." "What does derogatory mean?" "That means that's a bad name. They [Whites] . . . feel insecure and so the only way they can feel good about themselves is to make somebody else feel bad. So, they do that with Negroes, and they call you nigger." And so when somebody calls you a nigger, you tell them, "I would rather be a Negro than poor White trash!" That was the lesson we were taught before we went out the door to start school, and I was just waiting for an opportunity to say it . . . [because] for us, that was like armor. You know, it didn't make any difference about you calling us a nigger because I'd rather be a Negro than poor White trash.

This child's early lesson in the importance of resistance also illustrates the universality of racism and prejudice across age, class, and geographical boundaries.

The lessons in the psychological armor of resistance almost always included the notion that "You are as good as anybody else and don't you ever forget it." Parents and mentors taught that if children did their best, they could compete with anyone, regardless of color. One woman said, "[Mother] always taught us that we could do whatever we wanted to do if we worked hard at it. And I always felt, and again she always emphasized, that we were just as good as everybody else." Echoing the same sentiment, another said:

They [parents] would say, "Look at your achievements in school. All of you can play the piano. You sing well. And, you know, you're a nice kid. And you're very, very important. And don't ever let anyone put you down. If . . . anybody can do anything, you can do it better." And I always kept that in the back of my mind.

Not only mothers but fathers also taught this vital lesson, as one woman made clear in the following remarks:

He really would sit down and talk with us. We would just get together and talk maybe after dinner. And he always told us that, you know, "you have got a brain, so use it." He was saying to us that people just don't think. "They go put their minds in neutral and go where they're pushed. You better stand up for yourself. You've got what it takes, you've got to use it." And you know, he insisted on good manners. He said that good manners would take you to the White House. He said that first it has got to come from inside. You have to believe in yourself. He said that you've got to be strong within yourself, and then you can be strong with whatever that comes.

The positive self-esteem that resulted from such messages helped form an invisible shield of armor that served as a protection in later years when others attempted to demean their abilities and their sense of self-worth. They created a kind of emotional sanctuary. A Ph.D. in psychology summarized what her armor of resistance could do for her in these words: "So effective were my parents in making me feel that I was as good as anyone else that later I could find myself in a room of one thousand Whites all telling me that I was not as capable as they, and I would say 'No, you are wrong,' and really believe it."

"Always Be Economically Independent"

Paid labor has long been a part of Black American women's history. The historian Gerda Lerner says that Black women's relationship with work is best characterized not as "a liberating goal, but rather an imposed lifelong necessity."[6] The testimonies of these women reinforce her assertion. All recounted the importance of childhood lessons that emphasized work as a passport to economic independence. Some of their earliest memories are of parents who stressed hard work and the need for economic independence, even for married women.[7]

Work played a dominant role in family life. In most cases survival depended not only on both parents' employment but also on the contributions of the children themselves. But work was more than survival. In a way that was distinct for Black Americans during segregation, work was also resistance. It was a mechanism for teaching children values, such as hard work and responsibility, that would help them survive in a racist world. Parents from all social classes coached their children in this lesson. A retired social worker spoke of being expected as a teenager to look outside the home for a part-time job. Despite the relative affluence of her family, her need to be employed as a young girl underscores the ways that race and class intersected for Black families, making them more economically precarious than Whites. The jobs she could get as a Black girl filled her with a determination to get an education and to prepare herself for a different type of work:

> Well, before I finished high school, I started having little jobs. And most of the jobs that we had were taking care of rich White people's children. And I went to the mountains in the summer, you know, and earned money—that little bit of money they were paying. From Dunville, I would go to Beach Haven and take care of little White children all summer, and that sort of thing. And I knew I didn't want that to be my life work. I said, "Oh, no. I got to get above this."

Another woman remembered how her family taught her the importance of work and financial responsibility even before her teen years. She recalled:

> As a preteen and a teenager, my first job was helping my grandmother with her job. She worked at the medical arts building downtown as a custodian. You know, she used to have to be there at 6:30 in the morning. I used to go and help her. So that was like an early, early job I had. But one of the things that my mother always believed in, is that . . . children should work and they should contribute to the family. If I made two dollars, I had to take the two dollars home. Earn two dollars, take two dollars home, and my mother would say, "Okay now, I'll take out my part. This is for your room and board."

Many other women emphasized how very young they were when they began to learn the importance of work. It was not unusual for nine- or ten-year-olds to be expected to work for small amounts of money at whatever jobs they could find. They did weekend baby sitting or house cleaning for local White families. One woman explained, "When I started work at nine years old, I was making fifty cents an hour and that went on from the time I was nine years old until I finished school." Even as children, most of their paid labor was gender-specific, but sometimes brothers and sisters worked together as part of the family unit doing whatever was available to do. A woman who was the youngest of thirteen children (ten of whom graduated from college) told what her parents expected of them:

> All the other older brothers and sisters used to have to get up [very early]. My father, [a self-employed barber], also was a janitor at the bank—at two banks—which means that he went to work at four o'-clock in the morning. And the older children went with him to help clean up. That was before breakfast.

Just as the emphasis on the importance of work cut across all class boundaries, so did the stress on economic independence. Unlike affluent White girls of that time, who were expected to marry well and to become dependent on their husbands, Black girls were taught, regardless of their circumstances, to depend on themselves for economic solvency. As one woman said, "My mom did not stay at home, so it never occurred to me that I was supposed to marry and [have] my husband take care of me. I always saw myself as a working woman." The one physician we interviewed reminisced about the message her physician father gave her:

> My daddy used to say, and my husband would tell you [that] when we got married, he swears this is true . . . my daddy took him down to the railroad track and said, "Now, if you can't be nice to my daughter, you send her back home to me." But, in the meantime, when I told him I wanted to get married, he said, "Get married, but finish school. You must be independent." And his example was this, "Suppose something (and he was a great person for thinking about automobile accidents), . . . suppose you have an automobile accident, and he is crippled or maimed for life, who are you going to go to? Will you go on welfare, or are you going to be able to take care of things." He was very practical. But he didn't have to tell me, because I was going to do it anyway. Because those summers I was working, I was saving my money.

Another father, insisting that his daughter become economically independent even if she married, said:

> If by some chance you get married, I don't want a daughter of mine not knowing how to . . .support yourself. Cook and clean and do all

those things that they expect from a female, but, I also want you to be independent.

Of course, mothers also conveyed the message of economic independence to their daughters. Often, their entreaties were even more specific. A concerned mother is remembered as warning, "Have your children . . . [but] get your education first so that you will be prepared to take care of your children. It's a poor hen that can't scratch for a couple of biddies." Again, mothers, like fathers, did not see marriage as financial security for their daughters. Sometimes, as one retiree recalled, the messages from mothers reflected a tension between men's dominance and women's drive for independence:

> My mother used to always tell me, "You always work and have a little something of your own. Don't ever depend on anyone." And she said, "Even when you get married . . . don't ever give all your money—all that you make—to your husband. Always have a bank account of your own and be independent. Stand on your own two feet." And I've always done that.

Parents were not the only ones who stressed economic independence for women. One woman recalled her grandmother's constant admonition to her granddaughters: "Get so you don't have to ask anybody to be your daddy." When asked how she interpreted that message as a child, she replied, "I thought it meant what it meant. Yeah. Be independent. Do for yourself."

The family's concern that daughters always be able to take care of themselves is captured well in a statement made by a retired educator, who said:

> Even though they [parents] stressed being economically independent, they also stressed that if you married, you work as a unit . . . [however] you should always have something of your own. I'm not saying that you won't share your own with your partner. But just have something of your own. And I think that that's what they [parents] shared. It's ironic. My mother-in-law even said the same thing. She said, "You've got a good husband. He is my son. But you still

(because I didn't work when we first got married), you still need something of your own."

This testimony seems to carry a dual message. First, the warning about economic independence from a mother-in-law to her son's wife underscores how *all* Black American women were keenly attuned to the need for their economic independence, no matter what their relationship to men. It also seems to imply that while economic independence is important for the obvious financial security it brings, it also symbolizes one's separate identity apart from one's husband. In other words, be a mate, be a good partner, work as a unit—but maintain something for yourself that preserves your own sense of personhood.

Family life is important in the development of all children as they grow to become functioning adults in society. That minority families are faced with additional challenges and burdens is illustrated time and time again in the stories of these African American women. Growing up during segregation added additional strains. Yet, despite the hardships, parents demonstrated great creativity and strength in making a positive world for their children. They found ways to encourage their daughters to develop positive self-identities as young Black women who had to take control of their own lives.

Whether the themes highlighted are those that emphasize being the best or those that focus on the need to be economically independent, the accounts provided by the women interviewed underscore how race and gender intertwined to create and reinforce identities that were quite distinct from those of White girls of their generation. Their social class origins also influenced the directions their lives took and the experiences they had. Because they were Black women, they had to excel in order to reach a minimal level of success. They learned, too, from myriad sources, that self-reliance was not an option that they could call on if Prince Charming did not materialize—married or not, economic independence was mandatory. This was not just the lesson learned by *some* of these Black American women as youngsters; this was the lesson learned by *all*. Small wonder, then, that this message, so powerfully learned in childhood, remains a cornerstone of their identities, even in old age.

2

Survival and Resistance
Lessons in the Community

Every Black family in Riverville came to the train station to
see us off. There were two other Black kids out of my class,
so there were four of us leaving. And you know, not just the
parents, but the whole town, we're talking about maybe fifty
people—your aunts and everybody. Just about every family in
Riverville had somebody there. There was this pride and expectation . . . that you felt from everybody in town.
> (Retired special education teacher—youngest
> of thirteen children, ten of whom graduated
> from college—describing the day she and
> her brother went off to college)

If the family provided a strong foundation for the development of the women in our study, the broader community
only strengthened that foundation. It amplified familial lessons
and provided childhood experiences that are reflected today in
their adult lives. Key lessons in racial identity emerged from the
community and reinforced what they had learned in the home.
They saw people who lived, loved, and disagreed while still
being united in a common struggle to survive and resist the dominant White society. They witnessed the importance of sharing
talents and resources, and they observed that leadership took
many forms for both men and women. They encountered the
myriad ways that African American women engaged in critical

33

but unpaid labor for the benefit of their communities. In particular, they learned from firsthand experience that Black children had a special place in the community and that they were the responsibility of *all* its members.

The Black Community Remembered

Forty women told us that they grew up in urban or small-town neighborhoods. Ten grew up in rural areas. Thirty-two of the urban and small town dwellers and seven of the rural dwellers described their communities as segregated. Only eleven lived in communities that were even slightly racially integrated.

These women came of age in a time and in places where people not only knew who their neighbors were but knew their neighbors well. Parents knew one another, and they knew one another's children by name. They knew where they lived and what their parents did for a living. As one woman put it, "You knew everybody. You knew the people on Cambridge Road; you knew the people on Stevens—you knew about them, anyway. You knew what their names were. If somebody came to Cambridge Road to ask about somebody on Stevens, you knew." Rural areas were similar to urban in this regard:

> You know, people helped each other. People would just come visiting. There was no phone, of course, but people would stop by and there actually were quilting bees, and people helped build barns. They did all of that. People came and helped each other with their crops. Everybody was in the field; all the children were in the field.

A number of scholars, describing this era of segregation, have painted rich pictures of close-knit, highly self-contained neighborhoods where Black Americans of all social classes lived together.[1] Black businesses often thrived, thus minimizing the amount of trade that had to occur with Whites. Indeed, people could shop, attend church, go to school, and find entertainment without ever having to leave their communities. People from diverse walks of life lived side by side. One woman described her neighborhood as one in which there were "teachers, lawyers, doctors, all up and down those streets." Teachers, doctors, and lawyers lived close to barbers, janitors, and domestic workers. A woman who grew up in a sizable town, and whose father was a bath-house attendant and mother a dressmaker, remembered with pride that there were thirteen Black physicians in her community.

Status, however, had distinctly racial properties in Black communities. To some extent, race served to homogenize class distinctions by ensuring that status was not solely dependent on occupation—it could be earned in a variety of ways. While most African American women and men worked menial jobs by the definition of the dominant society, they were often accorded higher status in their own community because of their education, values, or contributions to the common good. Unlike in the dominant White society, professional status was not quite as important for community involvement, leadership, or recognition. Time after time, women from poor and modest backgrounds spoke of fathers and mothers who were "very well respected" and who played important roles within their communities. "Everyone knew my father and everyone knew my mother" was how one woman remembered the respect with which her working-class parents were held. Also, in contrast to their White counterparts, women played an important part in defining the overall social standing of the family in the Black community.[2]

Nevertheless, regard for those relatively few who were professionals was very high. Teaching was especially respected. Women, of course, played a particularly prominent role in teaching and were accorded very high status, because, as one woman said, "Teaching had a different connotation in the Black community." Blacks revered education and honored teachers who were responsible for developing the talents of a future generation of young people in whom parents placed much hope. Speaking from a child's perspective, another remembered how she and her friends "stood in awe of not only our neighbors but our teachers." Teachers were known to all in the community, and sometimes they even lived with families. One woman had a teacher live with her family for thirty-five years. In the words of another retiree who spoke at length on the subject, "Everybody in my community knew who the teachers were. The teachers went to church with you, knew your family and all that." Sometimes they were also the mothers, the sisters, and the aunts of these women or their friends.[3]

Occupying a professional position brought with it an obligation of service and leadership. "Everybody looked up to them" is how one woman remembered it, and another recalled that, despite their meager earnings, teachers were expected to donate "two days' pay to the old community chest." Teachers were expected to be exemplary role models. One woman underscored this point as she told how in her community a young female teacher had created an "uproar" because she behaved "inappropriate to her status," both as a woman and a professional, by going into a neighborhood bar. Older teachers in the community were particularly critical of her behavior.

In the specific case of women's leadership roles, the South's particularly well-established system of patriarchy dominated the experiences of Black and White American women. Black as well as White women's secular and religious leadership roles in their communities were constrained by traditional gender stratification.[4] As a consequence, the community contributions of these women were frequently taken for granted and thus rendered largely invisible—especially to the dominant society.[5]

In practically every community, certain individuals, mostly through their work contacts, had influence with members of the White community. They were considered community assets because they could represent the needs of others. Members of *all* classes were expected to use whatever influence they had with Whites to help other African Americans. Gender, however, greatly influenced whether these transactions with the White community were "frontstage" or "backstage."[6] In private negotiations with Whites, both men and women equally engaged in "backstage" negotiations. For example, a man or a woman might ask a White judge for a lighter sentence for someone who had run afoul of the law. However, if negotiations were of a more public nature, if the entire community had to be represented in matters such as voting or civic issues, Black men were the usual arbitrators.[7] Their roles were "frontstage." As the "race men," they used a variety of strategies that highlight the pragmatism with which Black Americans approached members of the dominant society.[8] One woman whose father's two jobs involved serving Whites—one as a barber and the second as a janitor in White physicians' offices—recalled, "My father made great waves quietly—he didn't advocate disharmony and things." On the other hand, the daughter of a trash collector described how her father spoke on behalf of the community:

> My father was the one who used to fight for everything in the neighborhood. [He would] yell . . . you know, when they had to fight to get the water in the neighborhood. Different things like that happened [and] he would have to go down to the courts and all and talk for the neighborhood and try to get this done and that done . . . and he was the one that knew [White] people, 'cause he got a lot of things done like that in the neighborhood.

The quality of life in Black neighborhoods was an important concern to the majority of residents, whatever their class or gender. One woman spoke for all when she said, "They wanted it to be clean; they wanted it to be safe." Such concerns required everyone to be watchful, to know not only the goings-on of their own family members but also to be aware of what others were doing. This level of familiarity was possible because, in so many ways, "everybody knew everybody." In a fundamental way, all members of these communities were engaged in "doing race."

A Place of Sharing

Common to descriptions of Black communities of this era is the ethos of sharing.[9] It infused these communities in a way that was distinctly racial and can be traced to the days of slavery. Individual and group survival often depended on this ethos, and it became a form of resistance to racism and oppression. So pervasive was the emphasis on sharing that it was often described as second nature.

In a way not true for Whites, economic vulnerability cut across class lines for Black Americans. The economic impact of segregation was felt even by Black professionals. For example, Black doctors and lawyers could sustain viable practices only as long as patients and clients could pay them for their services. Many took payment in the form of labor or food. Structural constraints forced all Black Americans to find ways, beyond individual endeavor, to subsist, to survive, and to endure. By combining resources, community members created a communal ammunition of resistance. The women we studied remember a life of sharing that was both a form of resistance to oppression and a celebration of humanity at its best. It went beyond the individual and was deeply embedded in the very fabric of the community.

Nothing is more basic to survival than food. Sharing food and other necessities with neighbors and friends was a daily practice. The pervasiveness of this norm is reflected in such comments as "Everybody shared from their gardens," or "If she didn't catch but two fish, she'd give us one, or "If you had a big pot of soup and you thought somebody else needed some of it, you handed them a jar," and "Whatever he [father] got from hunting and fishing would be enough for another friend and somebody down the street." The frequency and direction of sharing depended on need, as is illustrated by this comment: "It was a tight-knit neighborhood; they would share anything they had. They would see Mrs. James over there and she would have a lot of children, so they'd say, 'Well, let me send some food; let me send something over.'" The form of sharing, or "looking out for one another," as many women described it, depended on a number of factors, including class and gender. One woman from a middle-class background whose mother was a teacher described the kind of sharing that her family's resources and her mother's unpaid labor allowed:

> Our house was the kind that all the kids in the town could come to. Don't ask me how she [mother] did it, but there was always food, and she was a great cook and everybody came [to our house] . . . she could feed anybody at any time. And there were, of course, students that she taught that would always drop in.

Another teacher's daughter revealed that sharing sometimes went beyond food to include shelter and nurturing. She said, "Mama would keep a couple of students that were older, that went home on Friday afternoon. [They] needed somewhere to stay in order to go to public school . . . they lived in a rural area and would come back on Sunday night." This illustrates the role of women not only as teachers but as social organizers in the community. Such examples of sacrifice for a common good have stayed with these women into their older years.

So pervasive were the restrictions of segregation on Black Americans that even total strangers could avail themselves of the communal ethos of sharing. An example was given by one woman whose father was especially sensitive to the plight of Black Americans—even those he did not know:

> I remember [that] anytime in his travels [when] he [Father] would run into somebody kind of stranded—maybe they got in and the train had just gone—and he saw this nice-looking man and wanted to know if he could help him. And brought people to the house at midnight that he picked up at the railway station. And rather than take them to a boarding house because there were no Black hotels, and if there were, they would be a dump—and he would tell Mama, "You have to dress now . . . I brought so and so, and somebody's in the living room." And Mama said she didn't like it. And on Sunday he'd gather folks up from church and bring them home to dinner. . . . And Mama knew she'd always need to cook up plenty, and she couldn't have anything like steak or pork chops for dinner. She'd better have [laughs] chicken pot pie.

In this instance, one sees not only the relationship between structured inequality and the practice of lending aid to complete strangers but also the role that patriarchy played in the relationships between men and women. Men could be magnanimous in offering help, knowing that the women of the family would be expected to provide it.

The sharing of talent and skills was also a feature of these communities. The better-educated assisted neighbors who needed help filling out forms or dealing with complicated debts. One woman remembered that her mother "always had something to do [in the evening]. . . . I knew that she was always helping folks fill out their papers for mortgages. If they thought they had been overcharged, [she would] go through their bills with them." But those who were barbers, cooks, midwives, or carpenters often donated their time and know-how for the good of the community as well:

> [The community] had great pride in its school. . . . It was built by my older brother and some of the older men. . . . They had to go beg the county for money . . . and when they couldn't get but just a little bit, then the men donated their services and built that little four-room school.
>
> [My community was steeped in] this sense of caring, this sense of love, this sense of guidance, the sense of one for all, this sense that whenever there was a need, everybody rallied around. If somebody got burned out . . . everybody was there, and in two days they were back in the house—you know, with the community rallying, doing what you could to restore.

This sharing ethos also encompassed health care, since few people could afford to pay for hospital or nurses, even if such services were available to Black citizens. Women's unpaid labor played an important role and again illustrates how African American women were expected to contribute to community survival. Communities formally institutionalized women's role in the ethic of helping others, as the following statement demonstrates:

When I was a child, people did not spend long times in the hospital.
. . . And so people belonged to a lot of lodges . . . so when a member
was sick, the members of the organizations sat up nights with the
family. The family would go to bed, and a couple of ladies would
take charge of sitting half the night. Somebody would leave at twelve
o'clock, and somebody else would come in and sit. The community
tended to care for its own. Now, it's close friends and families, if anything happens.

Sometimes people's concern for others led to their involvement in very personal affairs of their neighbors. A woman who
admitted to growing up poor but "spoiled" as an only child remembered what happened in her family one Christmas. At considerable sacrifice, her parents had Santa bring her a desk and a
doll when she really wanted skates:

And I didn't really want a desk. I wanted skates so I could go out and
skate with the children. And the people of the neighborhood heard
about it. And my parents had spent what they had on the doll and
desk. You know, one lady—she was our neighbor [and] she said,
"Now, that child's got to have some skates." Because I cried and cried
and cried. And then the people of the neighborhood put in the
money, and she bought me those skates. And I will never forget it.

As this story indicates, children in these communities were seen
as belonging to all. This is probably the reason community members felt comfortable enough to involve themselves so intimately
in the family matters of neighbors. "You were everybody's
child" was how one woman summarized it. In contrast to what
Whites would likely define as outside interference at best or
doing an "end-run" on parental prerogatives at worst, community members could sometimes decide to preempt parental judgment, at least in selected situations such as the one described.

Special Concern for Children

The rearing of children was truly a community effort. Children "belonged to the people on the block," and neighbors were

responsible for one another's children. They watched over them and protected them from harm as they moved about the community going to school and church, running errands, and playing with each other. They also disciplined them as they would their own. However, this behavior was interpreted to the children as caring, rather than as interference; as loving, rather than as meddling. The socialization begun in the home was continued in the community by a multitude of surrogate parents.

The authority of adults was unquestioned and knew few class boundaries. One woman humorously remembered that in her neighborhood, "Even the drunks would look out for the children [by saying to them], 'You know your mama don't want you out here.'" The ubiquity of adult authority is captured in the words of another woman who said, "You didn't question it, you just didn't . . .it was considered the right thing to do." She went on to recount that children "probably didn't think about it at all." Another woman described it by saying, "Everyone helped each parent to raise their children." The nature of this relationship between children and adult members of the community is summarized in the following description:

> I remember having very, very good neighbors. Neighbors who were concerned about you and your family and about the safety of the children and about your behavior. [I remember] that you spoke to everybody. I don't care how many times you went down the street, you spoke. And you dare not do anything wrong because you knew it was going to come back to your parents. Neighbors were of the kind that would admonish you. If they saw you do something wrong, it wouldn't be, "I'm going to tell your parents;" it would be, "Viola, was that the right thing to do?" . . . And then, too, you knew that your parents were going to hear about it. Neighbors . . . were concerned about families and children as individuals. It was a tight-knit neighborhood; they would share anything they had.

Women played a pivotal role in their interactions with neighborhood children. The reminiscences of our interviewees illustrate some stark contrasts between their childhoods and those of most children today. The very young were especially singled out for protection from harm. One woman recalled that when they walked to and from school, "Mothers came out and stood on the yard and watched us and kept order and wouldn't let us fight." Women in particular were neighborhood disciplinarians and "would even whip other children if they were doing wrong." Not only would such physical admonition not be a source of confrontation between parent and neighbor; it was judged by both parties to be appropriate. The roles of women in the communities operated through the bonds of kinship and friendship.[10] One woman described it this way:

> And nobody fell out with anybody about anybody else's child. Anything that went wrong . . . Aunt Elizabeth came and told on you, that was it. There was no question about your wrongness. Whatever you did, [if] she said it, that was it. It isn't that my mother would have to go see, "Because my daughter said you grabbed her and you shook her," . . . there wasn't [any] of that . . . if she shook you, you deserved to be shaken. So, that's the way it was.

Furthermore, children understood that parents would reinforce each other's disciplining. If they knew that neighbors had seen them up to some mischief, "they knew what was coming when they got home."

Although women were the predominant nurturers and disciplinarians of neighborhood children, men, too, played a role in parenting and protecting them. That their involvement was often gender-specific is illustrated in the following recollection:

> We had a community center where we had dances every Friday night. And once in a while . . . some boys from the southwest, which was a bad section of the city at the time, would come over and create a disturbance. And my father was working at night at that time, and he would pass there and if he saw any disturbance, he'd come in and get us and at least ten more children. [He would say] "Okay, go home." And we'd go. . . . It was close like that. It was close in that my dad cut a lot of hair. He wasn't a barber, but he cut his own children's hair, and he cut all the boys that I knew around Cambridge Road. He just didn't charge them. He just cut their hair. If their parents gave him something, fine.

Communal parenting extended beyond neighborhood and community boundaries. Several women told stories about how they traveled alone by train as young children (sometimes as young as age five) on visits to grandparents and other relatives. Parents put them on the train and into the care of African American porters. These porters "looked out for them," seeing that they behaved, that they got something to eat, and that they got off safely at the right destination.

The African proverb "It takes a whole village to raise a child" was quoted by one woman to express her sense of how she and other children were raised by all. (This interview occurred before this expression came to national prominence through the publication of First Lady Hillary Rodham Clinton's book on the same topic.) The many conversations we had, as well as the writings of other scholars, support this as an apt description of how the members of these close-knit Black communities approached child rearing. Whether as youngsters or as teenagers, these women felt the watchful eyes of community adults on them. Their transgressions, their disappointments, and their triumphs were shared by people who knew them and cared about them. When their parents were not available, others in the community provided for them. Within their neighborhoods they had "homes away from home." When these women grew up and left their communities for new ones, they recreated much of what they had learned about the importance of community in their childhoods.

Community Tensions

Even though communities were cohesive and characterized by close bonds born largely out of racial segregation and racial persecution, tensions existed. The diversity of Black American community life had its strengths, but it also provided challenges. Heterogeneity created strains and sometimes disrupted community harmony. A number of women spoke of drunkenness, prostitution, and abusive relationships in their communities. These were facts of life. Differences in attitudes, norms, values, and approaches to life in various areas existed. As in the White world, good and evil, kindness and meanness were part and parcel of everyday life. Hence, there was never total consensus or complete unity—an important lesson for youngsters to learn. Tensions revolved around two major issues, both of which had to do with status, namely, differences in skin color and differences in lifestyle and values.

The issue of skin color was raised by women without any prompting. They spoke of skin shade or tone as a factor that often was divisive, even within their own families. Perhaps more than anything else, this issue illustrates the extraordinary power of race on the human psyche. For example, the darkest child in a large family remembered that her lighter-skinned sister would be taken for Sunday rides in her uncle's car—a privilege denied to her because she was "too dark." One day when her aunt and uncle came to pick up her sister, she asked if she could go also. This is the account of the ensuing conversation with her uncle:

> I said, "You never ask me to go." "Well, I tell you little girl, I don't let anybody any Blacker than I am ride in my car." And Aunt Pearl was sitting in the car, and I remember looking at her, and she laughed. She didn't say anything. She just chuckled, "Oh, Reverend Hawkes, you shouldn't say that." And I called him a real bad name. [laughs] I called him a real bad name! My mother never heard me say that in her life before nor after that, but she didn't whip me. I'll tell you that. She didn't whip me, which let me know that she concurred with me.

Much has been written about racial mixing since the days of slavery. Scholars have noted that light-skinned Black Americans were more acceptable to Whites and hence the most privileged, both economically and socially.[11] Many women recalled their family lineage going back to slavery. There was fairly frequent reference to the presence of both White and Native American ancestry. On a number of occasions, they showed family photographs that often visually reinforced this point rather dramatically. The women also concurred that, *in general*, light skin commanded a higher status and respect in both Black and White communities when they were growing up. Nevertheless, then as now, Black Americans' attitudes toward color cannot be easily captured or summarized; it was not a simple matter.[12] Light skin was not always a source of higher status. White stereotypes to the contrary, the women in our study gave little evidence that they yearned to be White or light-skinned as children (or adults). In fact, several women recalled being quite severely harassed by family members and neighborhood children for being so light. In one case, a retired educator who was the lightest in her family of fifteen children recalled how she and her siblings represented many different skin shades. She remembers going through what she called the "color phase" when she was teased unmercifully by siblings, often to the point of tears. Recollecting that pain, she spoke of the final insult from an older brother who told her that "She was left on the doorstep."

A second tension in the community revolved around differences in lifestyles and values. Some parents tried to isolate their children from peers or places that they considered potentially "bad influences." Legal segregation, and hence race, forced African American parents to live in specific neighborhoods, whatever their economic situation or aspirations. Thus, they found themselves unable physically to separate themselves from those elements that they wanted their children to avoid. The presence of diverse social types within a relatively small physical area presented a special challenge to them. For example, one retiree who grew up in a very poor neighborhood recalled how prostitutes lived next door to her family. She also remembered how her more affluent school friends "loved to come home with us because . . . they could see [lots of excitement], and we could peep and hear and see what was going on." Parents tried to prevent such associations by restricting their children's movements in the community. A retiree who grew up in a poor but upwardly mobile family told how her parents handled the situation:

And so we felt like we were better than the others. And then when we did go out to play, we came back with some bad words and so forth . . . and so, that wasn't the right thing, you don't use those words. . . . There was one other family in the neighborhood—a widowed mother who had two children that she was rearing, and they couldn't go outside to play or mix either.

Parents exercised control by carefully scrutinizing peers and, later, dates to ensure that they shared parental values.[13] One woman who grew up in an urban community told how her father would chastise her and tell her to go home immediately if he found her "standing on the corner." Others told how parents talked to them about how to select friends: "Don't be like certain people; be like others." Another recalled the following advice: "Don't spend three minutes with anyone who doesn't want education." Surrogate parents were equally concerned, as one woman described her grandmother [who worked as a domestic]: "She didn't let you associate with everybody."

Affluence meant greater success in controlling children's choice of companions. For example, a retiree who grew up in a prosperous, landed family in a small Southern town talked about her parents not wanting her and her sister to play "in the street." She mentioned specifically how such a decision was, for her parents, "a matter of control and selecting [our] friends." She continued:

But the reason we had croquet and basketball hoops and a net stretched for volleyball [was that] we owned the whole block that we lived in . . . we had plenty of space. So they [parents] tried to provide so that we didn't need to do much wandering. So, more children came to our house than our going to their houses.

In spite of these tensions, much of the essence of these communities was uniquely Black. Women gave accounts that underscore a sense of unity and oneness that was directly attributable to race. Their recollections, as well as the objective evidence provided by their later lives, also emphasize how the lessons learned and the values stressed within these communities were ones that would leave an indelible imprint on them. Their identities as African American women were forged within a milieu that stressed the common good, that accentuated the importance of "giving back" to one's community, that showed them that women had a special place in and responsibility for sustaining the community. The members of their childhood communities created a way of life that was much more than a reaction to White society. Its genesis, at least in part, lay within the moral and religious foundations in which these communities were steeped. It is to these foundations that we turn our attention in chapter 3 as we explore yet another important legacy in the lives of these women.

3

The Church
Sacred and Secular Entwined

> The church has always been important to me as a source of strength, really. And [then] there was the social side of church. You know, you met people there, and you were involved in some of the activities, the youth activities and that type of thing. And it was a big help, they gave in our church . . . [they] tried to keep everybody on the right path.
>
> (A Baptist and retired high school math teacher)

The church and its importance, especially in their youth, was a recurrent topic of conversation for the women in our study, and they shared many cherished recollections. Their childhood stories paint a picture that helps us appreciate the extent to which their lives were shaped by the legacies bequeathed by their churches. As adults, these women present a fairly diverse religious profile, but practically all of them were members of the Baptist or the Methodist church while they were growing up. The Baptist denomination was more popular than the Methodist, but those two denominations together accounted for most affiliations. This is not surprising in terms of the history of African American religion in the United States and the degree of local autonomy permitted by the Baptists and the slightly more hierarchal Methodist church.[1]

Racial oppression in general and segregation in particular ensured that the character of the Black American church was distinctly racialized. The Black church of these women's youth served as a sanctuary from White domination. As in slavery, churches and their ministers frequently served as agents of social change, particularly in the fight for racial equality.[2] To an extent not seen in White churches, spiritual or sacred concerns were meshed with the secular. Certainly, the otherworldly or spiritual aspects of the church—appreciation of God's word, attention to the Bible and its dictates—were influential parts of the church's power, but no less important was the attention given to the conditions under which Black Americans lived at the time. Martin Luther King, Jr., captured this duality of the church's mission when he said, "Any religion that professes to be concerned with the soul of men and is not concerned with the slums that damn them, the economic conditions that strangle them, and the social conditions that cripple them is a dry-as-dust religion."[3]

Scholars of the African American church have produced a rich body of literature on the church's significance within that community.[4] Recently, for example, Katie Geneva Cannon has reminded us that the aftereffects of Reconstruction resulted in the church's becoming the Black community's chief institution of power. In both rural and urban areas, the church was the major institution totally controlled by Black Americans. Cannon says, "It was the only place outside the home where Blacks could express themselves freely and take independent action. The church community was the heart, center, and basic organization of Black life.[5] The writer Gloria Wade-Gayles echoes this same sentiment. Speaking of the Black church, she says, "We designed it, controlled it, and made it work for us. It was the only institution in the community in which we never saw white supervisors, white inspectors—white people in charge. It was an empowering institution."[6]

Links among Church, Family, and Community

The connection among the family, the community, and the church was a hallmark of the Black American world in which the

women in our study grew up and came of age. Speaking specifically of the close link between community and church, one
woman said, "They [community and church] could not be separated. The community came through the door into the church,
and the church went out the door into the community." Quite
often communities bore the names of their churches, especially
in rural areas. But rural or urban, the people who filled the pews
on Sunday mornings were the same people these young girls saw
out in the community the rest of the week. The church, the community, and the school were largely made up of the same players. Children were bombarded by the same values and teachings
in different institutional settings, ensuring that there was little
opportunity to hear conflicting messages. One woman recalls
what that was like:

> And I can tell you that when you went to that church and then went
> to school, you met these same folks. My math teacher played the
> organ in the church . . . my English teacher was a member of the
> church, so it wasn't like I didn't see her anymore. We all lived in the
> same community. The schools at that time were segregated, and the
> neighborhoods were segregated so when you went to school, to
> church, the grocery store, you saw the same people. Their expecta-
> tions were the same, and they kept being reinforced.

From the pulpit they heard support for the values and moral
standards they had learned at home, and they witnessed the
moral condemnation of those who violated those values and
standards. The church provided role models whose lives they
could witness everyday.

The link between church and family was just as strong. Socialization begun in the home—the emphasis on basic familial
values of honesty, truthfulness, morality—continued in the
church. It was there that children found justification for what
they had been taught by the family.[7] Parents pointed to the scrip-
tures, to the word of God, to the teachings of the church, and to
the sermons of the minister as definitive, supportive evidence
that what they had been teaching at home was absolute and

grounded in spiritual truth. It was not just "do as I say because I say do it," but "do as I say because this is what Jesus would have you do." It is right. The Bible says so. When speaking of church and family, comments such as these were frequently heard: "We had strong religious values—had a strong sense of right from wrong"; "Religiously, we were taught to say prayers and to respect God, to observe the Sabbath"; "You know the scripture they used was, 'In all thy ways acknowledge Him, and He shall direct thy path.'" One woman summed it up this way:

> You had to do the right thing. It doesn't matter what other people say, you just go on and do what you think is right. And it's stood me in good stead. And it was a matter of praying when you opened your eyes, and praying just before you closed your eyes, and "Stay close to God, and He will see you through."

The Centrality of the Church

Clearly, the church was the most important form of organized life in the community during the childhoods of these women. It was the hub around which life was organized. People's weeks were largely structured by church activities. As one woman said, "The church was a major part of my life as a child. Sunday school and church activities, you know, going to something at church two or three times a week." Saturdays were filled with preparation for Sunday—getting clothes ready to wear, cooking, and doing anything that needed to be done to avoid labor on Sunday because "On Sundays, you did nothing. You could not. If you had to do it on Sunday, it could have been done on Saturday, and why wasn't it?" Sunday was for church and little else. Over and over again, we heard comments like these: "Saturday you prepared for it, and then up on Sunday and go to church"; "Everybody left my house Sunday morning and went to church"; "When you were young, you didn't have any choice. Mama went to church and when you got up on Sunday morning, you knew you were going to church. Rain, sleet, hail, snow, it didn't matter"; and "We were expected to get up on Sunday morning and go to Sunday school. We expected to go back to Temple League or BYPU or something, because on that day, Sunday afternoon, we'd go to the youth programs at several churches."

Sunday was holy. The only activity approved with any certainty on that day was church activity. Time and time again we heard comments such as, "You couldn't go outside and play outside on Sunday. It was the Lord's day. Regardless of how you might have felt on Sunday, you had to get up and go to church." Another woman laughed as she told how it was:

> As a youngster, in order to go out in the afternoons to the park or to the movies, you had to attend church that morning. If you were too sick to go to church that morning, you were too sick to go out to the park [laughing] or the movies or whatever that afternoon or later in the evening. So I grew up getting up and going to church.

In practically all cases, mothers and fathers were united in their emphasis on church attendance for their children. This is not to say that both parents attended church themselves, although that was certainly the norm. However, in some instances the mother remained at home, too tired to attend services after getting the rest of the family ready and off to church. And in other cases, fathers had jobs that required that they work on Saturdays and Sundays. It was also not that unusual for mother and father to belong to different churches, that is, one to the Baptist and the other to the Methodist. In these cases, the children were expected to owe primary allegiance to one or the other, but they also divided their church time between the two, albeit somewhat unevenly. Sometimes children found their time spread thin among several churches as they tried to meet varying expectations:

> I had a godmother that was a school principal, and she was a member of an African-Methodist church. Of course, I got involved in her church activities being on programs there. My father was a choir master and the Sunday school superintendent of a Baptist church.

And my mother was a church clerk of a Methodist church, and my best friends belonged to the Church of God and Christ and they had a lot of nice youth activities. So in that circle, I was around doing on the programs, you know, making speeches, in little plays, and so forth.

In short, church attendance and participation were expected—even demanded—of these women. This was true even for those who did not perceive their families as being particularly religious in the spiritual sense, as evidenced by such comments as, "I wouldn't say they were very religious, but they were church-going people. When we were growing up, if you didn't go to church, you were considered bad people. [laughs] In other words, you don't associate with those people because those people don't go to church."

Social Life of Youth in the Church

A number of women spoke of the place of religion in their lives as "a source of strength," as "an anchor," or "as something beyond me that kept me going." However, not a single woman ever described the religion of her youth as focusing on the hereafter rather than the present. This is interesting in view of the fact that a common stereotype about the function of religion among the dispossessed is to distract them from the woes of the present life by teaching them how much better things will be for them in the hereafter, especially compared to those who have it good in this world. It is true that we did not specifically ask about the kind of theological teachings to which they were exposed as children; still, when given the opportunity to discuss the importance of the church in their early lives, no one even alluded to or hinted at such a purpose. Instead, while clearly recognizing the importance of the church as a spiritual anchor, most of the women focused their comments on the church as the scene of their social lives.

The church was the center of social life in the community for both adults and children. It was there that they met friends and neighbors. Ostensibly they came together for worship, but much more than that took place at church. Friendships were formed and renewed, compliments and gossip were exchanged, dates were arranged and carried out, meals were served and consumed, emotional support was offered and received, and acknowledgments for achievements were made and accepted. The church provided entertainment through the presentations of music, readings, and dramas. Often, recreational activities were organized by the church. As one woman exclaimed, "The church was the hub of activity. There was no community center." But perhaps a retired college professor and civic official summarized it best when she said:

> No question but that the church was the social center. You could meet your boyfriends there and court real good. I am serious! I am serious! You knew who was cute and who was not cute. You knew whose mama would let them do certain things. And you could get the best information, you know, like the good gossip like who was going with whom. It was better than the beauty shop. I didn't go to the beauty shop. My church was my social center in terms of exchanging information, in terms of what was going on, in terms of who was in trouble, in terms of who was beating their wives, and who was failing in their grade . . . any information you wanted. We did not have the Black newspaper then, so we just went to church. You could get it all [there].

More Blending of the Sacred and the Secular

The existence of the church as the major empowering institution for Blacks in a racially segregated world afforded it the opportunity to take on a variety of other secular functions.[8] It provided the first opportunity for economic cooperation among Black Americans as they pooled their resources to purchase property and to build churches. Mutual aid societies also grew out of the churches. They became sources of assistance for Black Americans in times of sickness or death and were often the germ for the growth of secular insurance companies. Furthermore, the church encouraged and promoted educational opportunities.

Many women talked about how such church activities operated in their family lives and communities. Certainly they realized that the values and codes of behavior they had learned in the home had their bases in religious teachings. They also recalled that the church served economic as well as religious functions. They spoke about the church's making small emergency loans to members in need, and they recounted how their mothers contributed to savings clubs that were paid off at the end of the year in much the same way that White banks paid off annual Christmas club funds.

The Church as a Shaper

But the church also provided opportunities for children to grow and to develop in other ways. Two particular aspects of the church stand out in the memories of these women—and both reinforce the fact that the Black church reached far beyond the spiritual domain. The first, already discussed, concerned the fact that the church was a critical social center that shaped their young lives on a weekly basis. A second powerful contribution made by the churches of their youth involved the notion that it was within the shelter of the church that they first developed and practiced their leadership skills and gained self-confidence. There they could hone the skills taught in the school and reinforced in the home. The church gave them a chance to speak before a supportive and loving congregation. Writing skills were learned and practiced as they translated Bible stories into plays and pageants, which they then performed for appreciative and supportive audiences. Speaking fondly of her church community, a retired educator said:

I mean they liked all the children . . . everybody loved me. They thought I was going to be something. Yeah, it was a shaper. It was, you know. I knew everybody in the church loved me. I think the Black church doesn't do what it used to do. You know, the church really totally embraced you, and they always thought I was good at whatever I did. People always applauded you, and they told you were wonderful . . . you know, that kind of thing.

The skills and strategies necessary for survival in a White-dominated, racist society, fostered in the family and community, certainly continued to be honed in the church. Indeed, the church prepared youngsters in a fashion that could not easily be accomplished in other settings. For example, learning the importance of discipline and of heeding the authority of elders who were practiced in survival in a racist society were especially critical skills for young Black Americans in this era.[9] The reminiscences of one woman suggest the implicit role played by the church in teaching self-restraint and discipline to youngsters:

You learned what was expected of you as a member of that community. They didn't have nurseries. Children just learned how to sit in church and to be quiet because if you did not, someone would lean over and look at you, and that would be the last straw—then you would sit up tight—I mean real straight. So it was where values— what was acceptable—it was a whole molding experience in the church—not just in Sunday school class, but wherever there was an adult in that church.

This description, which harks back to an era without nurseries where children are free to play and have fun, captures a trial of self-discipline that young children were required to practice for hours at a time. More important, it alludes to the overwhelming power of adults to command behavior that today would be considered well nigh impossible.

The church of these women's youth also provided an arena in which to practice skills and to gain experience that would serve them well whenever they went out into the world beyond their homes and communities. Confidence-building endeavors such as public speaking and performing, writing, and debating public issues were key elements of what the church provided. Under the watchful eyes of church elders, the women also rehearsed the social graces and the rules of etiquette for good behavior. In a way, the church afforded them a stage for experiential learning, one filled with loving and reassuring spectators and mentors. Here one learned to stand before an audience and sing or speak. There were plays to write and to perform. Programs had to be organized, developed, and executed. Leadership skills were sharpened; poise and confidence were nurtured and instilled. Of course, the schools played their part in this type of development, but to many, what was begun in school was practiced and brought to maturity in the church. It was the church that became the showcase for their talents. A well-known civic leader said of her early church experiences:

> I had more practice in church than I did in school. They had more opportunities for you to stand up and say your little piece. I can't remember my first little piece, but I remember thinking, I wasn't scared because I had said it over and over and over. If I had stumped my toe, I would have lost my whole spiel. But I remember standing up thinking, "Ummmmm, I am not even scared; I am saying this before all these folks." I was so proud of myself. But then, later in life, when I ran for public office and had to stand up before all those people, you say GOD! But then it all comes back to you—those first experiences stand you in good stead.

She continued her testimony to the church as she said:

> I got my speaking experience in the church. I was telling my son the other day that people don't understand, that you learn a sense of identity, a sense of self, a sense of poise, a sense of appreciation. The teacher let me teach Sunday school. I thought that was very important. I didn't know much, but I could read my little verse and read my little lesson, and I could help teacher. When she wasn't there, I could take over. So I learned. You could develop leadership skills. People learned to trust you. You could take up offering. So you got up-front roles and responsibility. And you learned a sense of self con-

fidence in the church. Particularly on the third Sunday. That used to be youth day. The young folks would sing, take up the offering, make the announcements—everything except the sermon and prayer.

Teaching Gender Scripts and Racial Protest

Still other kinds of conduct were fostered in the church. Many of these were gender-specific and reserved only for girls. The complexities of deference that were central to normative notions of feminine behavior—deportment, manners, and protocol—were reinforced and learned in the presence of stern religious glances and raised eyebrows. One woman remembered "people of the church" admonishing girls who were just beginning to date to "keep your legs crossed while on dates." She recalled:

> We didn't have charm schools and all that sort of thing. This [the church] is where you learned how to be a lady—that's what they used to teach you in the church—some things you don't do, like you don't laugh out loud, you don't chew chewing gum, you don't wear your hats in the house, and you are to be respectable.

This description of appropriate behavior appears on its face to contain a number of admonitions that could apply equally to girls and boys. Yet, on closer examination, we discern the double standard contained in the moral admonition that sexual purity was especially required of women in order for them to be considered "respectable."

The church taught other lessons remembered as being more racial in nature. These were lessons for survival in the outside world—lessons that were equally appropriate to all African Americans, men and women, rich and poor. It taught them the value of organizing, of coming together, and of advocacy. It taught them how to resist the injustice of the system while obeying the letter of the law. The following lengthy comment illustrates such lessons:

I remember when our neighborhood wanted to get sidewalks. We wanted to get the streets paved, because when it rained, they would get muuuudddy and track mud in everywhere. In the summer it was so dusty and black that when you would raise the windows, you would get a thin coat of dust all over everything. We rallied around the preacher. We attacked this; we demanded that, and we went down town [to city hall]. We did not get it, but we knew how to come together, though. So I saw the church as an organizing force and as a place that built unity. It was good; we had some good stuff. That's the place, too, where they told us that you obey the laws. Don't break them. I remember when we took this ride downtown on the back of the bus. The law said that you ride on the back of the bus, but Reverend Tatum said as the seats get vacant, you just move to the vacant seat, and don't move, for as long as you are in that seat, it's your seat. And this was back in the forties. Ummmm, you could move forward as long as they [the seats] were vacant. When the bus came to our neighborhood, there were still White persons on it, but as it left the neighborhood to go back around, they got off. Now we could sit in their seats. When you get closer to town, White folks would get on, but Reverend Tatum would say, "Don't get up because it was your seat. You had paid the price; you sit there." And nobody was going to say anything because by then you would have a busload of Black folks. But when you first got on, you went all the way to the back. You start in the back. But I learned that in church—that first political procedure, that first advocacy, that first empowerment piece they call it now. But he [Reverend Tatum] said, "You are just standing for what's right—obey the laws; don't break the laws—'cause they would have whipped the crap out of us. It [the church] was a laboratory for living. It was a laboratory for living, and [the preacher] would preach about it, too.

In its own way, then, the church reinforced the norms of the larger Black community. The armor of survival and resistance forged in the home and community was bolstered in the name of God. By preparing and practicing its young parishioners in skills and behaviors needed to function well in the world both in and outside the Black American community, it was giving them a shield of protection, reinforced with confidence and laced with pride and a strong sense of identity. They went forth knowing and believing that they were people worthy of respect because they respected themselves.

Gender and Class Tensions

The overlapping memberships of family, church, and community made for an extraordinary degree of closeness and cohesion in the church, but those features did not preclude the presence of tensions. Gender and class tensions that existed in the community spilled over into the church. The patriarchy that operated in the homes of the larger society extended into the sanctuary. Bernice Barnett has also pointed out that the patriarchy that was so prevalent at that time structured the experiences of both Black and White women.[10] Indeed, in retrospect, many of the women we interviewed recognized the gender asymmetry that was pervasive in their churches. Men were the power brokers in their churches—they commanded the "front stage" of church life. By contrast, the women of the church were relegated to the "back stage," to the caretaker roles expected of women. Consequently, our interviews were full of reminiscences about how mothers really did most of the work, yet fathers, brothers, and uncles occupied the visible positions of authority. The women were the ones who taught Sunday school, sang in the choir, played the piano, arranged the flowers, cleaned the building, cooked for church socials, and occasionally clerked for the church, but it was the men who served as deacons, trustees, and ministers. Men were the ones who controlled the money and called the shots. How this played out in terms of gender hierarchy is conveyed by the description one woman laughingly provided of her own parents' relationship to their church: "Mother worked in the church a lot. She was just sort of a church worker. . . . Now my father was the head of the church. You wouldn't get a minister or anything there unless you had to pass him. He was a deacon and chaired a lot of committees and that sort of thing."

Despite a normative order that dictated women's deference to men, some women sometimes felt strongly enough about an issue to openly challenge male authority and to publicly chastise male leaders.[11] A grandmother and an aunt are remembered proudly by one woman because they stood up to the deacons of the church whom they believed to be wrong in their treatment of the young minister. The deacons wanted to get rid of the minister because he played tennis, which they believed to be sinful. While waiting to take formal action, the deacons nailed the church shut to keep the minister out. Outraged by their behavior, the two women decided to confront them, as the following account shows:

> The deacons nailed the church up! Nailed the church to keep the preacher out. Grandma and Aunt Bess rented a truck. I was right along with them. They rented a truck, took their axes and their handkerchiefs, and went up there. Two women. That's right. I don't know exactly how it resolved itself, but I remember she [grandmother] got up in church, and she pointed her finger at the deacon, and said, "You're crucifying that young man just like the Jews crucified Jesus Christ." I never will forget that.

A different example of gender inequality within the church was provided by another woman who vividly recalled a story that highlights the blatant and humiliating discrimination some women suffered:

> I could not understand why if a young woman got pregnant, she had to be paraded down front in the church and confess her sins and then be put out of the church. It seemed to me that would be a time when the church would rally around and be supportive. I could never understand that, and I haven't yet. But it never happened that the man who might have been responsible was ever put out. It was always the woman.

At other times, tensions in the church were class based. A woman brought up in a North Carolina town said that in her church there was a "difference in terms of class" and that the elite also tended to have light skin—so light that, with light hair and blue eyes, some of them could have passed as White. Of the class differences in church, she had this to say:

> These were the folks who lived down on Pacific Avenue, Pennsylvania, Maryland, and Caroline [avenues]. That's where the mortician lived—the minister lived on Pacific—the doctors lived on Pacific. We lived on Virginia, which ran perpendicular to those thoroughfares. But they attended the same church as the rest of us, but they were the deacons, the trustees—the power brokers in the church—no question. And for the most part, these were the college-educated folks. If not, they were like Mr. Rainer, who owned the grocery store. These people had trappings—real good trappings.

Trappings aside, the emphasis on race uplift work served as an important vehicle for uniting the Black community. The same woman went on to illustrate this point:

> The church linked and connected us in terms of sense of community, because even though there were different social classes, there was still a sense of community. If there was an issue, if, for example, we had to go down to city hall—the church would be the place for our community meeting. And the minister, he was really good, he would be the person who would advocate for us in terms of going downtown.

As we look back at the description of their early lives in the church, we gain appreciation of the ways that these women were shaped by this religious organization. The Black church of segregated America operated within tightly confined boundaries, ones that set it apart from White society and even from White churches of similar denominations. Within the church, Black Americans could assemble, organize, and exert power and leadership without being subjected to the scrutiny of the dominant White society. The church of their youth not only ministered to the spiritual needs of its members but also addressed secular needs—most important, in fighting for racial justice.

The memories of these women reinforce these ideas but, in a very personal way, they also capture another powerful aspect of the church's contribution—it provided for their social welfare. This aspect of the Black church of their youth is especially noteworthy because other outlets for social organization were scarce. The absence of multiple avenues for social life and socialization gave the church special power to influence the lives of its young members. One woman captured what many alluded to when she referred to the church of her youth as a "shaper." The ways that the church molded their lives were many and complex. At the simplest level, it provided a venue for a highly supervised social life—for meeting and greeting and having good times. At another level, the church and its ministers had a lifelong impact on these women by encouraging a strong ideology of personal responsibility for the betterment of their race. In other ways, the church served as an arena of experiential learning for its youngsters. And finally, at still another level—one more implicit and taken for granted—the church supported the gender codes of the larger social order by reinforcing and reproducing women's inequality.

4

Education
Passport to a Better Life

[Being Black] had a bearing on my desire for education. I had
an inculcated desire from early childhood to have a college
education because I was Black. I always had the understanding. [It] became a part of me from a very early age that I had
to do better because I was Black.

> (Retired senior government official whose
> parents moved her family North for
> improved educational opportunities)

The restrictions and the stumbling blocks that the
women in our study faced in life made education especially crucial for all of them.[1] One woman summarized a common sentiment by saying, "I think that it would be safe to say that the feeling was [that] education held the key to success in life, and without it, you couldn't—you wouldn't be able to get very far."
Again speaking to this notion of education as a vehicle of mobility, a retiree said, "You knew that education was the way.
[There] was no doubt about it, and there was no reason [ac-
cepted] why you couldn't succeed."

Racial hierarchy generated conditions that hindered Black
Americans while providing automatic privilege for Whites. Consequently, Black Americans needed more education. A woman
from a family of modest means and ten children, seven of whom
completed college, provides insight into why education was so
critical for those who hoped to improve their situation in life:

You see, in the Black community, education was the stepping stone. But that [was] not true in the White community because they did not have to go to school to get good jobs. They didn't have to be overqualified. They could go because of the legacy or who they were, and could go into business. They could get loans and this sort of thing. Black children did not have those options.

Another put it this way:

Black people knew that in order for any of us [boys or girls] to make any kind of living, and to make our way in the world, we had to have some kind of training, some kind of education because the opportunities were so limited that even with a degree, the opportunities were so limited that you just couldn't think of not having some kind of skill—some kind of training—some kind of education. Otherwise, all you could be would be a maid. A man could be a chauffeur, a gardener, an elevator operator—some kind of domestic work or janitor—something like that. There were very few opportunities.

Education represented both a survival tool in an inhospitable world and a strategy of resistance to those who would deny African Americans the advantages that the educated enjoy. Even though education might not pave the road to the American Dream as many Whites would experience it, its absence virtually ensured a life of manual labor for Blacks. For Black American women, lack of education would mean working in two kitchens—a White woman's as well as their own. A woman who worked while in high school with her mother for a White professional woman recalled what stimulated her own desire for an education:

And I knew there had to be something in life that was better than what we had. I was not afraid to work to do better. [Mother] didn't have the opportunity to go to school, but I did. In high school, I worked for one of the ladies that Mom worked for. You know, I saw the kind of home that she had, and she would tell me what her work was—And I liked what I saw, and I wanted something similar to what she had, and to do some of the things that she did.

In this case her exposure as a young girl allowed for a firsthand comparison of White privilege and Black disadvantage. With hindsight sharpened by a lifetime of negotiating inequality, her words point to the reality of racial inequities. She knew education would improve her situation, but it would not give her everything that it gave White women.

Parents and Surrogates as Motivators

Early emphasis on education was forcefully instilled within the family. Almost every woman we interviewed recalled how she was given the message that she must do better than her parents. As one woman put it, "Mama said that every generation should be a little better off than the previous." Being educated meant the chance for a lifestyle free from having to work so hard, free from manual labor, free from having to work weekends. Another woman reminisced, "My mother was doing domestic work, and she always said, 'I want you to have a better life than I had. Therefore, you must go to school.' And when she said, 'You must go,' you must go, and you must behave yourself. If you ever had a [bad] report from the teacher, then you were really in bad shape." Several others provided memories that show how education was stressed in their families:

> They [parents] were anxious that we would complete school as much as we could. They always wanted us to be able to do better than they had done. They stressed a college education. I think I sort of wanted to go to college anyway. They, you know, provided me with as much help as they could, and so I went by aid of scholarships. But I would see things that I wanted, and things that I wanted to do, and I knew I had to, you know, go to college and all to accomplish some of those things.

> She [Mother] always wanted me to be a very successful person. This was demonstrated by her behavior, her caring manner, her high ideals. She just wanted me to do more than she had done because she

always felt that she would have finished college if her father had not died.

They [parents] taught us the value of education. I always knew [that] my parents expected me to go to college. It wasn't do I want to, [or] if I'm going to—I always knew that I was going to do that.

In my home growing up, it was no such thing as you're not going to college. Yes, it was always taken for granted that you're going to go. I'm saying the attitude of both my parents was just always when you finish high school, you go to college, and for them, you go on to graduate school. Now, neither of my parents went to college.

Even for the minority of our respondents whose families were affluent, doing better meant getting a still better job, having more security, and maintaining their positions of leadership in the community.

Perhaps the most outstanding behavioral reminders of the great importance of education were the kinds of sacrifices that parents made and that children themselves were expected to make. Walks to school were often long, and winter nights had usually fallen before children came through the kitchen door. Occasionally, public schools were abandoned for the promise of better opportunities in the Catholic parochial schools, and children had to leave neighborhood friends and cope with strange and different settings. The hardest sacrifice for both parents and children, however, came when children had to leave home in order to continue their education. This happened most frequently when the rural area or small town in which a child lived had no schools for Blacks beyond the elementary level, so the child had to move to another town and live with relatives during the school week. Or it might happen that the child would have to move to another state and see parents only on holidays or vacations. For the affluent few, boarding school was the option most often chosen. Today, as adults, they understand and appreciate the sacrifices, but, as little girls, they found these separations difficult. Parents prepared them for leaving home by reminding them of the importance of education and by pointing out their lack of opportunities at home. They were reminded that relatives loved them enough to take them in and that they would be missed at home. With the wisdom of hindsight and accomplishment, the women say that, even as children, they understood and appreciated the sacrifice they were being asked to make. Still, their stories ring with sadness. Consider the case of a little girl who at the age of seven was sent to live for two years with an aunt in Philadelphia. She remembered "going into the dining room after my mother left and standing by and touching the chair where she sat whenever she came to visit. It always made me feel better to do that. Somehow, I felt closer to her."

Assuming the responsibility of rearing other people's children was one not taken lightly by relatives. These surrogate parents were careful not to make mistakes that would get them or their wards into trouble. In taking on the role of parental surrogate, they were often more demanding and stricter disciplinarians than the child's biological parents would have been. For example, a woman who grew up in a poor rural family lived with a cousin in New York so that she could attend school. She reflected on her years away from home:

> Mother wanted us to have opportunities, and she knew that she and my father could not afford those opportunities, and she was very happy that we had relatives who could help. Looking back over it, it was a great opportunity because you know, I often look back over my life and say, "Now, had it not been for that cousin, and then later another cousin, where would I be today?" It was a great opportunity; it's just that the life that I remember living in New York with my cousin was not a very happy life. She [the cousin] knew very little about raising children. She provided me with lots of experiences, you know, cultural things that I would not have probably experienced. What she was doing was great; it's just that every little thing that I did, I was punished. And punishment then was to go to your room. Looks like I spent more time in my room looking out that one window than I did doing anything else.

The practice of living with other relatives in order to obtain an education did not end with graduation from high school. A number of women also lived with relatives while attending college or graduate school. In some instances, the relatives provided not only room and board but tuition and fees as well. A woman from a poor background was sent to boarding school by a prosperous uncle and then later lived with him in order to attend college. Reflecting on those experiences, she remarked, "It happened in many [other] Black families, too—that if people get ahead, it is very often that other family members have supported them and worked together. The older ones get out and then they help some of the younger ones—aunts and uncles help." Her statement provides evidence of how survival was a group strategy within the Black community and family and illustrates the ethos of racial uplift in operation.

As mentioned earlier, in rare instances an entire family would pull up roots and relocate in order to provide better educational opportunities for their children. This happened to one woman when she reached high school age. Her father took a job in a Northern city and the family moved. She remembered her father saying, "'The children will get a better education, and they will be in an environment where they will not be segregated, and the opportunities for them will be better.' And so that's why he took the job. My mother cried." Even this kind of sacrifice, however, was not without mixed consequences. Attending integrated schools in a racist society was seldom a positive experience. Children who had such experiences found themselves in predominantly White schools run by White principals and taught by White teachers. Black role models outside the home were nonexistent. The familiar support system of family, community, and school working together in the best interest of the child was missing. In such a situation, the family bore the responsibility alone. The following incident from the life of a little girl who attended an integrated school in the North makes this point. The White teacher has just discovered that her Black student wants to become a teacher. Here is how the teacher responded:

She said, "Mosel, have you seen any colored teachers? There are no colored teachers. Have you seen any colored teachers?" I said, "No, I haven't, but my mother and father said that I can become whatever I want to become!" I said, "And I'm going to become a teacher." So she said, "Well, I wish you luck, but you'll never become one."

This little girl went on not only to become a teacher but to earn her master's degree and to be awarded an honorary doctorate. A strong family support system, combined with the self-confidence that had been fostered within her family, sustained her when she was confronted with the cruel and demeaning comments of her White teacher.

Beyond the sacrifices made by mothers, fathers, aunts, and uncles, a number of women from large families were also indebted to older siblings who contributed their resources toward the education of younger brothers and sisters. Where families were too large and too poor for all the children to attend college, it was usually the younger ones who attended, mainly through the efforts of the older ones who had left home and gone to work. Consequently, a later birth position in a large family was correlated with attaining a college education. On the other hand, if only one child from a two- or three-child family attended college, it was likely to be the older one. The women felt that this was due to the responsibility placed on the older child in the family to be a good example for the younger children. Also, the older child was simply forced to be more responsible in terms of looking out for the younger siblings. A typical comment highlights this phenomenon: "As the first child, I felt the responsibility that I had to sort of lead the way, or be an example for my sister and brother." Another comment shows us how survival and the drive for success became a group strategy for these Black Americans: "As each child left home, Mama and Papa never said, 'I expect you to come back and help with the next one'; it was just something we knew we were going to do. Each one came back and helped the next one get through." As older siblings, many of the women participated in this pattern of be-havior. Sometimes it was done at considerable personal sacrifice, as revealed by the following remembrance of a woman from a very poor family:

> My [younger] sister finished college before I did. [I] never shall for-get. She was going to join the army. She was going to get into the ser-vice if she couldn't go to school when she first graduated from high school. Anyway, I told her that she could not join the army. I would help her go to school instead of my going to school. So the little bit of money I saved for me to go to school, I gave it to her, and we got her a loan, and she went directly to college after finishing high school. Whereas me, I didn't get a B.S. until 1960.

Aside from financial assistance, other kinds of family support were given. A number of women spoke of receiving help with homework, of the presence of advocates in the school and at PTA meetings, and, of course, of emotional support. Mothers were especially helpful. In ways that illustrate the taken-for-granted nature of the unpaid labor so typical of women, they re-called not only mothers sitting with children around the table at night encouraging and offering help but also mothers attending the PTA meetings, going on school trips, cooking for special out-ings, and sewing the costumes for school plays. And it was moth-ers who held hands, offered shoulders to cry on, and believed in their children's potential when others doubted. A retired school teacher who went back and finished college late in life attributes much of her perseverance to her mother:

> When everybody laughed about [my] going back to school when I was so old, she [mother] said, "Elizabeth, you're going back to school, so don't worry any." And then she said, "If I, if we can help you in any way, we will." Always I'd come home from school, and she'd say, "Well, you don't have long now, and that's one thing I am looking forward to—to see you walk across that stage and get the diploma." And the disheartening thing was that I graduated in May, and she died in April. She didn't live to see me graduate. One month. That made me very sad. It most certainly did.

The insistence on education, the efforts to motivate, and the collective family support did not go unrewarded. The desire to succeed academically was firmly implanted. For many, these were difficult years of sacrifice and struggle. Only the most affluent avoided working to help defray the costs of their schooling. Some delayed the completion of degrees until middle years, but, in the end, the key to the door to a brighter future was obtained.

Forty-nine of the women in our sample completed some college. Forty-one went on to do graduate work—many at enormous sacrifice to themselves and to their families. In the end, the sacrifices paid off. Twenty-four hold master's degrees, and nine have doctoral degrees. Most of the women attended segregated Black colleges in the South as undergraduates, but a large number went to other sections of the country for their graduate education. (The most frequently attended Northern universities were Columbia University, the University of Chicago, and the University of Michigan.)

Other Sources of Motivation

While parents were mentioned most frequently, teachers were also remembered for their ability to motivate with their compliments and their special recognition of students' curiosity, creativity, or initiative. The women also occasionally cited their spouses, at later points in their lives, as providing encouragement during their graduate school days. For one of the oldest women we interviewed, it was her grandfather, who had been born into slavery, who became her chief motivation: "Well, I got that [motivation for education] from my grandfather because he, well, when I first knew him, he couldn't read nor write. He had [been] in slavery until he was twelve years old, and he always thought that you ought to have an education." For another, it was her middle-class peers:

I would say, more than anything else, those factors which determined my strong desire to attend college were my peers that I ran around with. I happened to have been involved with a small group of young people whose parents were highly professional people and who seemed to have had more material things than I did. It's just the way things worked out. My best girlfriend's mother had attended college. Her father had a very successful barber shop. And we had another friend in our group whose mother was a successful music supervisor for the school system and whose father was an employee of the postal services. It was something about those young people that I had chosen for my friends, and we had been friends for years, and all of us were going to college. And all of us did.

This narrative illustrates the social class asymmetry that was inescapable for Blacks in segregated America. Denied access to the broader economy, they found economic opportunities to be severely curtailed. Jobs that would have been considered less than professional status in the dominant White society were given elevated status in the Black American community. Thus, we hear fathers who were storekeepers and postal workers spoken of as "highly professional people."[2]

Although people were generally referred to as sources of motivation, specific experiences and events also played a particularly memorable part in some women's lives. More often than not, these were negative experiences that could be escaped or avoided with the help of education. A woman who earned a master's degree and ended her career as a senior government employee has vivid recollections of the very moment when she decided that she had to get an education. Her family was very poor, and, as a young girl, she worked part-time for a White family for whom her father and mother also worked. Typical of the sorts of work girls did, her job was to watch the family's children. She was also expected to clean house, make beds, and do dishes while she did her baby sitting. The following incident occurred one day as she was washing dishes for her White employer:

I was washing dishes that morning, and she [the employer] came through the kitchen. I was looking [out the window] because I could see our house in the field from her house. And she said, "Estelle, what are you planning to do after you finish high school?" And I said, "I don't know." And she said, "I know you don't want to wash my dishes and your dishes the rest of your life." And I said under my breath, "Hell, No!" And that Monday morning, I got on the school bus, rode those twenty-five miles to school, and jumped off at that school and ran to the guidance counselor and said, "Miss Barker, I want to go to college!" And she said, "You do, sugar?" "Yes, Ma'am!" That was a life-turning event. Oh, absolutely! Because all that I knew that we had available to us was working in somebody's house.

A successful guidance counselor recalled what prompted her to return to graduate school. She had taken a job right out of college. One look at her first paycheck sent her back to get more credentials:

And I got my first paycheck, and I thought that I would be able to purchase an outfit. I only could afford to pay layaway, [laughs] and that took all of my check. I worked a week, and that's when I said, "Oh, No! This won't do." We started looking at how much money we made without an education, and how much we made with an education, and it wasn't hard to convince me.

Both of these recollections support what one woman gave as a primary reason for the importance of education in the lives of African Americans. She said, "I think they saw education as important because that was the road to financial gain, to material possession, to better your position in life." Although they had probably heard this many times from their parents, these women's personal experiences in the world of work drove home the importance of education in a very special way.

Instilling Pride in Self and Race

"You're as good as anybody else" was an important lesson begun in the home but continued and reinforced in the school. This message was repeated by teachers who "were caring of us, and [who] did everything in their power to encourage us." Some remembered "[a mother who] had books with strong Black role models, and grandparents [who] told wonderful stories about Black life." Teachers "who had authority and knowledge" carried on that tradition by teaching Black history. They spoke about the accomplishments of Black people down through the centuries. They broke the silence of White children's secondhand textbooks with regard to the place of Blacks in American history. They extolled the virtues of Black literature, poetry, inventions, and scientific achievements. They read from the works of Black authors, brought Black newspapers and magazines to the classrooms, and convinced many of their students that they too could become all of this and more. A retired high school guidance counselor had this to say: "Yes, you were taught that you were the greatest. You felt that you were somebody. You were going to succeed whether you were in business or going on to college. That part you were taught; you were somebody. It was an assumption." These lessons were the armor that helped ward off attacks such as the one remembered by a woman who walked to school each day. She remembers vividly how, one day, a bus loaded with White children passed by, and the children leaned out the windows calling, "Nigger, Nigger, Nigger!"

In addition to having developed a sense of racial pride, practically every woman to whom we spoke said that her self-confidence was developed or enhanced because she was made to feel personally special by someone. This label sometimes came from very unlikely sources, as illustrated by the following story from a woman now in her eighties:

> My sister's supposed to have been very pretty, and I was supposed to have been this ugly little fat girl. And let me tell you what kind of experience I had. Nobody knows when I learned to read, but a woman came to our house selling magazines or something. As soon as I got a magazine in my hand (I must have been five; I hadn't started with school), I began reading it. And she looked at my mother and said, "Is she reading that?" And my mother said, "Oh, yes, she is reading that." And she said, "Oh, she's an ugly little thing, but isn't she

smart." [laughs] Now I remember that, and I really think that maybe that was the first compliment I had about being smart. [laughs]

More typically, compliments were less backhanded and came from someone in the family. "I think that I was considered to be a kind of a family star. I think the expectations for me were communicated by my sisters and by my father" is how one retired university professor remembered it. Another fondly remembered compliment came from a stepmother who is recalled as "the most influential person [in my life]. She always made me feel that she knew that I could achieve whatever I wanted to achieve. She was forever complimenting, praising, encouraging, so that you got the feeling that I can't let this lady down."

More often than not, the designation of being special came from a teacher. This is not surprising in view of the fact that the distinctive feature of most of the women was their intellectual ability. Time and time again, we heard "I was smart," "I was considered smart," "I always took first honors," or "I skipped two grades." Since teachers were perceived as the last authority in recognizing intellectual promise, such notice was taken seriously. If a teacher said you were special, then it must be true. Teachers usually recognized especially gifted children while they were quite young and still in grade school:

> So I never felt that I was all that special until I was in the fifth grade. I was behind because I had started late. One of my teachers said that I should go to summer school. She thought that I was smart enough that I could skip. So I went to summer school, and they skipped me. And then I went to summer school again, and they skipped me.

For some, however, recognition of intellectual prowess did not come until much later. One woman said of a college experience, "We had an instructor—the man that was the chairman of the department. God! He made me feel like, you know I was just wonderful. [laughs] I tell you; I'm just wonderful!"

Now and then the feeling of being special was born out of pain. The exceptional trait itself might have been the cause of the pain until some sensitive person put things in perspective. For example, we heard one account of how being smart was a cause for great unhappiness until a caring teacher turned the situation around:

> I'm really just being very honest with you that it was very painful being the smartest child in the class or the brightest child at the school. It was very painful and hurtful, and people did all kinds of unkind things to you. When it was snowing outside, they [other kids] took your cap. And then [it hurt] being called teacher's pet.

This same woman went on to explain how her seventh grade teacher used cards with students' names on them to decide whom to call on for recitation. She shuffled the cards and then selected one at a time and called on each student in turn. This woman was always ready with the correct answer. Of course, the fateful day arrived when she gave an incorrect response. Her classmates laughed in glee at her mistake. Then the teacher intervened and restored her pride and self-confidence. This is how she remembers it:

> [The teacher] made me feel like king of the walk. By the time she got through telling them off, "If the rest of you would just answer just one fourth of the lessons she does—and you've got the nerve to laugh at her because she misses one!" I mean, I would tell her until she died, when I would see her at church, I would tell her about what she did for me as a little girl. That stands out. That stands out because somebody came to my rescue.

Others held tightly to what made them special, namely, being smart, as a compensation for less desirable traits. A woman of light complexion was often teased as a child by her siblings. This was very painful, but there was nothing she could do to change the situation. Finally, she chose the best revenge, which was to shine intellectually. She said:

> I had one sister and one brother who would call me yellow. And I would cry, and I'd tell my Mom because Daddy was down at the other store. He'd come home late. Mom would get after them, but then they would get me around the corner, twist my arm and things like that for telling on them. But I knew that when I was about ten

that I was a special person in my family. I knew I had to live beyond all that. I knew I had an excellent brain, and I knew I was good when I hit the books, and so I couldn't worry about their doing that.

Being special—being smart—set these young girls apart. They felt different because of it, and they were sometimes aware of how it influenced their self-identities and their destinies. Explaining how this awareness affected her life, a retired college professor related:

Well I knew, I felt very early that I was going to have to be different from most of the Black girls in Marketville. I wanted something that was different. Many of them were getting married early or having babies before they got married, and I didn't want that life for myself. I had not been encouraged to have that kind of life, and it made me strive harder so my life would be different. Because I had been a good student, I never had a problem with [obtaining] money for studying—always had a fellowship of some kind.

This woman went on to earn a doctorate from Columbia University and enjoyed a successful college teaching career. She epitomizes the life path of those who became convinced that education was the key to a good life, who were motivated and supported in their educational pursuits, and who knew that they were special enough to accomplish their goals and aspirations.

Black Schools and Black Teachers Remembered

Although the church occupied center stage in the Black American community, the school stood not far behind. It did not enjoy the autonomy, independence, and total freedom from White dominance and interference that the church did, but it did operate as a semi-independent institution. It was subject to policy decisions set by White school boards, and Black educators had little control with regard to matters such as budgeting, hiring, plant facilities, and general curriculum. However, Whites were generally disinterested in what was taking place in Black schools on a daily basis. Consequently, Black Americans ran the internal affairs of their schools pretty much as they pleased. For the most part, their world of education consisted of Black school principals, Black teachers, and Black students.

Black American teachers were highly respected and were of vital significance in their communities.[3] One woman reminded us that "Teaching had a different connotation in the Black community. They [teachers] were a part of the community. They were the leaders, and the community looked up to them for whatever was going on in the community." Teachers lived among the students they taught. They knew the parents, and the parents knew and respected them. Education of the children was considered a partnership among parents, teachers, and community and church members. Because of housing patterns imposed by segregation, Black school communities included a spectrum of social classes, and their members were united in their support for teachers and schools. All came together at PTA meetings and volunteered their respective skills and strengths in helping educators motivate and educate their children. Although many parents were not formally educated themselves, they revered education and what they thought it could do for their children. They lent their assistance in ways that they could by helping with special school programs and field trips and by seeing that their children attended school without fail.[4]

Segregation of schools meant inequality on a variety of fronts for Black Americans. Physical plants were inferior to those in White schools in terms of size and quality. Gymnasiums, music rooms, and cafeterias were rarely found in Black children's school buildings. Books and supplies were not plentiful and were often hand-me-downs from the local White schools. A retired college professor and administrator conveys her sense of these differences:

> Our books came from the White school. You understand what I'm trying to say? We had used books from other White schools. And you know for a fact that the facilities were not the same. When White

kids were being taught, they had typewriters; we didn't have any typewriters. It took us some time to even get business courses in our schools. We started out, as far as I'm concerned, behind in terms of resources and opportunities.

Schools for Black American children were also less numerous, and they were seldom conveniently located. Walking long distances was common for even very young children. Traveling to school by bus was something denied to many Black children: "See, I started off to school in the country, and we lived near some people who were White. Of course, there were children. They rode the bus, and we walked to school. That was a difference right there." In addition, counties and small towns rarely had schools beyond the elementary grades for African Americans. Black children who wanted more than was provided by their home communities had to be educated elsewhere. As we have noted, this meant leaving home at an early age to live with relatives or friends in a larger community where public education was available for Blacks. It meant attending the only private schools families could afford. More often than not, these were Catholic parochial schools, which taught religious beliefs very foreign to the families of these southern Protestants.

If segregated Black facilities were second-rate, the perceptions of teachers and the quality of instruction were anything but inferior. Many conversations focused on how genuinely committed teachers were to the best interests of their students and how they repeatedly went beyond normal expectations by teaching more than formal academic requirements. In ways that were especially gendered, women teachers were often more like surrogate parents, like "other mothers" to their pupils.[5] These teachers—as women and as representatives of the middle class—were interested in the total education of their students as social and moral beings.[6] A woman who wanted to become a physician but settled for teaching because "We didn't have any doctor money" remembered the importance of teachers in the lives of students as surrogate parents and as teachers of racial pride:

Along the way, we had good teachers who encouraged us to get as much education as we possibly could, and we had extremely good teachers. We lived in I guess what you could say was a poverty-stricken area, and there were many kids who didn't get a chance to go to church on Sunday. So on Friday, we would always have Sunday school lesson. On Monday, we had history. We would have, I guess you would say, Georgia history. On Wednesday, we would have Negro history. Anyway, she [the teacher] almost acted like a mother because when you were ill at school, she always had some little mixture to give you to make you feel better, or sit you over in a corner where you would be real warm. She took a lot of care of us. That's where I first learned about Black history. She used to bring in the *Pittsburgh Courier*, which was a Black newspaper. She would bring that paper to school so that we could get it, and we could read.

Speaking of her segregated school experiences, still another woman commented on how Black women teachers as representatives of relative privilege saw it as part of their duty to do race uplift work: "This goes back again to the sense of community. Etiquette was taught; dress was taught; manners were taught; religion was taught; morality was taught, and all of that."

The notion of the school experience as a joint community endeavor was commonly expressed. As one retired college professor said, "The pattern of other adults taking an interest in children, you know, was quite prevalent." Teachers and parents worked together like hand and glove. The presence of teachers in students' lives extended beyond the walls of the school, as is illustrated by the comment, "Oh, yeah, sure, everybody in my community knew who the teachers were. The teachers went to church with you, knew your family and all of that. And it was just more, 'I feel responsible for you.'" The effectiveness of these overlapping group memberships in motivating and controlling children's lives can be seen from the remarks of a woman from a family of fifteen children who went on to get her doctorate in education:

We dared not act up in school because the teacher lived in the neighborhood, went to the church, and they would certainly tell on you, [laughs] you know? And motivate you. They would say, "You're a Morgan. I know you can get it." "A Morgan; I know you are not going to act up." They would say to somebody younger, "You are not going to act up because I'll tell your older sister. She's right in the next building." Or, "I'm going to tell your mama when I come to the store." [laughs] You know that kind of approach.

To the extent that parents' education would allow, lessons at school were reinforced in the home. Again, mothers were more frequently cited in this regard than were fathers. It was the mothers who were most likely to be surrogate teachers:

We had good teaching at home. In addition to the school teaching, we had the teaching that my mother did—you know, teaching us to speak. If you had a part in a play or anything, or debates, she wanted to know what your points were. She said, "You need to make three good points. You've got to be ready for the rebuttal." And she would go into another room and say, "I can't hear you." Then, in addition to that, churches had such good youth programs. I mean, there wasn't anywhere else to go but to church and the youth programs. We had Christmas plays and that sort of thing. So, you know, I learned to speak—that was a result of that participation from elementary school on, you know, with the home and school working together.

Another woman underscored comments like these and emphasized the fact that some of the mothers were well educated themselves:

My mother was the scholar, and so from a little girl, she sat right with you and taught you what you had learned in school that day. She re-taught you. And when I was in kindergarten, they were into phonics. That was 1935, but they were into phonics, and we'd get a sound a day. First we got the alphabet, then we'd get a sound every day. And I'd come home and tell mother, and mother would put it down, and then she'd combine the sounds and help you come up with words. And then when I started getting a word a day, she'd combine the words and help you come up with a story with the words you learned.

Limitations: The Impact of Race, Class, and Gender

In spite of all the emphasis on education and all the entreaties backed by family and others to go further—to become someone, to make the Black community proud—everyone recognized that there were limitations on their futures. The boundaries imposed by race, class, and gender formed the matrix within which African American women sought to satisfy their aspirations. Well before completing high school, the women were aware of just how narrowly defined their career opportunities would be. They recognized the multiple jeopardies in being Black and female. Over and over again, we heard the refrain, "Teaching, nursing, and perhaps social work. That's what we had open to us. That's what educated Black women could look forward to." A retired school teacher lamented, "Oh, Lord yeah, I could only be a nurse, a teacher, or a housemaid when I started out. That's all I could be—do general housework, teach, or nurse. You weren't in on everything. No, women were not in on everything—Black women especially."

If Black women "were not in on everything," poor Black women were in on even less. They were even more limited in career choices due to their meager financial resources. Regardless of ambition, they had to be realistic. Many times that meant attending college or graduate school in their home towns or those of relatives. If the profession or specialty they preferred was not taught in the local area, they had to select from what was available and open to them as Black women. In discussing her career choice, a lifelong educator told how race and class had conspired against her: "I wanted to be a nurse at one time, but the local medical school was segregated. We couldn't go there. I would have had to go some place else, and I certainly couldn't afford that." Another educator had a similar story to tell: "In terms of opportunities, I think it was very much limited to teaching and nursing and clerical. As a matter of fact, I thought in terms of nursing as a career and had been accepted, but wasn't able to go because we didn't have the money. So that's how I happened to sidetrack."

Even "on track," however, women could still look forward to gender discrimination. A retired physician remembered how it was for women in medical school:

> One of the professors who taught chemistry, he was the one that told us girls had no business in medical school. They ought to be home in the kitchen. That was the one ugly thing I remember. I just thought he was there to teach us, not to preach and tell what his idea was. He wasn't on the admissions committee. It was none of his business, but you couldn't say anything, you know. You just had to sit there and swallow it. There were five of us [women] in the class.

Gender discrimination was not limited to professors in the classroom. Fellow students did their share to make women feel uncomfortable and to let them know they were overstepping the bounds of acceptable behavior and to "cool them out" of their desire for advancement. Discrimination existed not only against those in "male" occupations but also against those in "male" specialties. In a story that illustrates the resentment that these women faced—even from Black males—a woman told how she was treated by her male peers while attending graduate school at the University of Michigan: "I want to tell you something. If I ever felt segregated against as a Black female, I did by the few Black males. They treated you like you had the plague. They might just smile and nod their head politely, but they didn't engage you in any conversation."

Had these women been made to feel welcome in traditionally male professions and specialties, would their lives have been different? Would they have pursued different careers and experienced different lifestyles? We can only speculate that they would have, on the basis of comments such as, "I think being a female is the reason I went into teaching, because otherwise, had I been a male I could've done some other things." And a former guidance counselor mused, "If I had been male, I probably would've been a lawyer—or a doctor—probably." She went on to tell how her best friend in college was a man who is now a very well-known author and attorney. They had always competed for grades while in school, and she had usually beaten him. She wonders now what life would have been like had she had his opportunities: "It just never occurred to me that I could become a lawyer."

On the other hand, there are those who believe that, had they been men, they might not have gotten as much education or become professionals at all. Some felt that because their options in life were more limited, they were more likely to stay in school than were men. One woman who did not complete her master's degree until after she married said:

> If I had been a man, I probably would have given up. Maybe I'd have found a job making pretty good money and would have given up on education. Probably would have. I am pretty sure of it, because when I first started teaching my husband told me he was making more money than me at the hospital. He looked at my check and laughed at it. He said, "I think maybe custodians are making more money at the hospital than my wife."

The chances of high educational achievement were favorable for those fortunate enough to be from loving and supportive families and communities that encouraged them to strive and to excel academically. Within the constraints placed on them by race, class, and gender, the women weighed their options, made their choices, and persevered toward their goals. While some may look back with nostalgia and wistfulness and wonder about how things might have been different, one thing is very clear—they do not look back with any sense of having squandered opportunities. All of them take pride in the fact that they did their best with the cards they were dealt.

5

The World of Work
Making It the Hard Way

I prepared my work, and I enjoyed doing it. Of course, some
of the children sometimes make you feel like killing them.
Nothing bothered me more than to have a child with a good
brain [who did] not use it. I was concerned about that. And
then I was concerned about the children's home life.

(Retired elementary school teacher)

[Had I been White] I don't think it would have been as difficult for me to get jobs. Well, I know that [because] I would
be called for an interview sight unseen and then rejected on
sight. I know that there were many jobs that I could have
gotten had I been White. I could have gotten better paying
jobs. (Retired university administrator
who worked a variety of jobs)

I think my whole life was sex discrimination because as a
Black female the only area for employment was teaching
where you could get a decent salary. And yet when I started
teaching I made $2,500 a year [in 1954].

(Retired school administrator)

The previous chapters have illustrated the various
lessons of survival and resistance learned by the retirees in our
study during their childhood and youth. In this chapter we shift
focus and concentrate on their work world. We begin by exploring the ways that race, class, and gender constrained their

employment and career opportunities. Their stories of challenges in segregated and integrated environments help us to fathom the extent to which racism and sexism prevailed. We come to appreciate that these Black American women faced adversity without being consumed by it. We are reminded of the extent to which the legacies of their younger years served to guide, console, and fortify them as they pursued economic independence.

The vast majority of the women in our study got jobs and developed their careers during three decades. Ten women went to work for the first time in the 1930s, twenty-seven in the 1940s, and ten in the 1950s. Thus, most (forty-seven out of fifty) shared a common historical location prior to both the civil rights and the women's liberation movements of the 1960s that controlled their career options and formative work experiences. They faced structural constraints that were both pervasive and uniform. Affirmative action and other government programs to counteract discrimination did not exist before the mid-1960s. Likewise, there was no public language to describe gender discrimination. Consequently, conditions were not significantly different for these women, regardless of the decade during which they entered the labor force, making cohort analysis fairly meaningless. With their career paths shaped by widespread racism and sexism, all shared a similar level of oppression and discrimination.[1] The first part of this chapter deals with the work lives of these forty-seven women. We take a separate look at the three women who began their careers in the 1960s.

Limited Choices

In step with the social geography of the time, the majority of the women we interviewed began their careers in teaching (thirty in all), most of them at the elementary school level. Five other women began their careers in other female-dominated professions—two in social work, one in library science, one in nursing, and one in dietary science. Only one woman, whose father was a physician, began her career in the male-dominated profession of medicine. In addition, not all began as professionals. Twelve began in jobs that carried little or no prestige, such as domestic worker, restaurant worker, secretary, or clerk.

Even though some women spoke of youthful dreams of entering law or medicine, most were aware of the limited career options open to them as African American women. "There weren't too many fields that were open to us then" was a much-repeated phrase. Teaching, nursing, and social work were almost exclusively the career opportunities available to college-educated women, especially to women of color. The explanation of one woman's decision to be a teacher puts a human face on these realities: "I didn't want to be a nurse, I was really interested in becoming a doctor, but if I couldn't be the real thing [I'd become a teacher]."

Accounts of their early career days illustrate a keen awareness of the restrictions imposed by race. In contrast, gender constraints were largely taken for granted and were relatively invisible to them.[2] As one woman explained, "Sexism just didn't play a role [in how we saw things] at that particular time," and another mused, "Back then we were not into the gender thing." As these women recollected their career choices, we see the extent to which gender restrictions were taken for granted. One woman, among the very top students in a very competitive college preparatory class in a Northern high school, recalled: "I was preparing to be a teacher. If I had been a man I probably would have been a lawyer or a doctor."[3] As we further explored how race and gender influenced her career path, she allowed that as a young woman she was very conscious of how her race created impediments, but it had never dawned on her that she had been limited in her choices also because she was a woman. Today, of course, awareness of sexism and women's inequality unavoidably influences how a number of them reconstruct their pasts.

Working in an African American Environment during Legal Segregation

Thirty of the women we interviewed worked for the majority of their careers in predominantly African American settings. Even though such work arrangements offered them respite from many of the daily personal assaults of a racist society, it did not remove the reality of racial inequities. Salaries were depressed for Black American professionals, as they were for the Black population in general.[4] The consequences of such restrictions are apparent in the comment of a retiree who spoke of how, "When I saw the Black attorneys, they were all in these frayed white collars, all frayed because they were so poor." The only medical doctor we interviewed also reinforced this point. Throughout her career as a physician, she had worked exclusively with African American patients. As she discussed the timing of her retirement, she commented, "If people would have paid me what they owed me, I could have stopped [earlier]. But that wasn't the point. They couldn't pay, they didn't have it."

Race and gender were entangled as vehicles of salary inequity. Men were paid more than women, and White women were paid more than Black women. In one instance, a former teacher told us that she started teaching for $2,500 per year in a county where White women started at $3,500. Another recalls how, in her early days of teaching, she worked in the evenings as a domestic worker for two White women who were also teachers:

> Even after I was in the school system, I worked in the evenings. Because my younger sisters and brothers had to have car fare. And I went to work for these two teachers, and they used to ask me questions, "Where do you get the energy to come and work for us in the evenings? And we do the same thing that you do and we're so pooped out." But, you see, you do what you have to do. And that little change that they paid me, I gave it to my sisters and brothers for bus fare.

Here we get a strong sense of how race influenced the status of this teacher. Because she was African American and was paid less than Whites, her profession did not provide her an adequate income to meet her family obligations. Yet, as she pointed out, the White women teachers could afford the "little change" it took to hire a Black woman to do their housework.

Several other women told us that they had avoided teaching precisely because of its low pay. One woman explained her choice of social work by telling us, "I didn't want to be a teacher. I said, 'Good Lord, they [don't make] money! You'll starve to death teaching!'" As one of them summed it up, "You know, I was interested in making more money. All the time. That's why I [would] leave jobs. I don't mind saying that [laughing], I'd leave for more money."[5] Despite their low salaries, however, the female-dominated professions of teaching, social work, and nursing provided something else African American professional women had to have—economic independence through a steady and reliable income.

Educators Doing Race and Gender Work

Because the majority of the women started their work lives as teachers, their formative work experiences were rife with the inequities spawned by a racially segregated system. Scholars have documented repeatedly the details of the inferiority of public schooling for Black Americans during legal segregation.[6] The human side of these discriminatory policies are less well documented, however. The reminiscences of these women fill some of this gap and provide an appreciation of how their everyday work lives as teachers were shaped by inequity.

Two conditions overshadow the stories we heard about the challenges of teaching during segregation—large classes and woefully inadequate supplies. The words of one woman who began her teaching career in 1948 describe the conditions: "When I first started teaching, I stood up and looked at forty-two children. Now that was a difference between the segregated schools and the integrated schools—we never had less than thirty children." The same woman, who taught for forty-one years, went on to recall what it was like to teach fewer children once her school was integrated in the late 1960s. "I had twenty-five children—I'd never seen just twenty-five. And I said, 'This is a picnic.'" When it came to supplies for the children, teachers remembered how they bought them out of their meager salaries. Responding to a question about her sense of how things would have been different for her had she been White, a former teacher said, "I would've had more supplies to deal with and [I] wouldn't have used my own money for supplies. We did that for years. Bought our own—pens, paper, and anything else that we wanted the children to have."

But there is a positive side to this story of large classes and inadequate educational facilities that Black Americans suffered during legal segregation. Although well known within the older African American community itself, it is mostly untold in the dominant White society. From many different examples drawn from their youth and from their work lives as educators, a powerful story emerged during our interviews with these women. It is the story of the numerous positive effects born from this unjust system.[7]

Despite all the drawbacks, teaching offered racialized and gendered aspects that provided great satisfaction to these Black American educators. Respect for teachers was high in the Black community, which mitigated some of the negative aspects of work conditions. Teachers were revered, not only because they were professionals at a time and in a place where most were not but also because they were professionals who could provide Black American children with the education they needed to make dreams of a better life come true. In a very real sense, teachers were vehicles of class mobility. The words of one former teacher capture this idea: "When I first started teaching, the parents were glad for us to try to teach their children the things that would make them better. If you were a teacher you were highly respected." In a paradoxical way, Black American teachers also enjoyed a measure of freedom in the classroom that was unavailable to most Whites. For instance, while Black schools were subject to White policy on matters such as budgets, plant facilities, and general curriculum, they escaped White scrutiny of their everyday operations. This meant that Black teachers had a certain autonomy that allowed them, for example, to teach Black history. Undetected by White eyes, they could give their students that special attention they felt their children needed in order to have any chance at all in their lives. These aspects of life as professionals provided them with a strong sense of satisfaction and reward and allowed them to carry on the tradition of survival and resistance. The genesis of such fulfillment was intimately tied to the oppression of the broader African American community. Race was indeed a key. As Patricia Hill Collins notes, "This culture was a culture of resistance, essential to the struggle for group survival."[8]

A major strategy in these teachers' fight for the survival of future generations involved what scholars have called "uplift work" or "race work."[9] Some felt that as women, they were more sensitive than men to this facet of their work. As one woman put it, "Men didn't have the sense of mission [we women had]."[10] For women, a key dimension of their jobs as teachers was preparing the next generation to survive in a racist society. Another was to provide the children with the ammunition they would need to resist the negative messages from the dominant society. A third aspect was the drive to provide young people with the educational tools that would allow them to prosper, to be upwardly mobile, to move toward a better life than their parents, "to make something of themselves."

Some teachers spoke of their duty not only to confront but also to dispel the negative stereotypes that were held by the dominant society regarding Black intelligence. One woman touched on this directly when she talked about how hard she worked to make her students excel: "We dogged those children and got the best out of them. When I say dogged, I mean we dogged them. Stayed on them." Referring specifically to the dawning of desegregation, she continued, "I knew that our Black kids were going

to put the lie to what White folks had said, because we had graduated many, many good students." Another woman alluded to
the same issue when she said, "It wasn't right to see talent
wasted, potential wasted. We cared. We knew the road, and we
insisted that they work up to their potential. We drove them."
The allusion to a common road is an important one because it
speaks to a common foundation that characterized the Black
American experience and created the conditions that ensured
that gender and class took a secondary status to race.

These teachers' concerns for their students' chances in the
broader community reflected their social class and gendered locations. Reared in communities where they themselves were
treated as children of the community, where the family extended
into the community and the community embraced the family,
where teachers were required to visit the homes of their students
several times a year, it is hardly surprising that these women
teachers became surrogate mothers to their students. For example, if children from disadvantaged members of the community
were not taught the basics of hygiene and personal care at home,
teachers took it on themselves to teach them at school, as the following comments illustrate:

> When I first started working, conditions were extremely poor. Chil-
> dren would come to school unkempt. Finally, I decided [that] I would
> get a washcloth and soap. We had a little washpan that we were sup-
> posed to wash the board with, and we would get water and the kids
> would go in the bathroom and wash themselves up.

> I bought clothes for many [students], shoes and underwear [too]. I'll
> never forget one girl came one day and we were having a play. And,
> of course, when [she] bent over [you could see that] her pants [were]
> just like that floor there. So I went to the office, asked the principal if
> I could send somebody up to a place called Troy's, a discount store,
> and get something to put on her.

Others spoke of how they taught children good grooming by
telling students, "Your hair needs combing," or "You need to
change clothes after a bath." A former teacher summarizes,

"Black teachers taught everything—etiquette, dress, and manners"; as it was put by another, "[Black] teachers taught a kid, not a subject."

A number of former teachers spoke directly about or alluded to the human element of their work, that is, how they taught children, not just subjects. This in no way implied that academic content or rigor was irrelevant. As one woman put it, "Black teachers knew from whence the Black child came. They knew the Black experience and had a vested interest in seeing that that child made progress, and that child knew it."

It was important to them that students knew they cared. The philosophy was that cared-for children responded better in the classroom. A former teacher explained, "Children know if you care. You know, you don't have to say, 'I care about you.' It's your facial expressions, your touch, the way you talk. They know that." What is strongly hinted at, but not explicitly spelled out, in all these comments is the fact that all Black Americans—whatever their class, gender, or position in life—shared a feeling of unity, a sense of togetherness or community born from a common oppression. This meant that in the specific case of teachers, they served as a bridge between an oppressed group and the meritocratic social structure.

As previously mentioned, it was not unusual for these women to claim that they approached their jobs differently from men. They felt that Black women teachers took on different types of responsibility from their male counterparts. One woman who taught especially poor children not only remembers how she and other women teachers paid attention to concerns beyond the academic but also suggests that such attention separated women from men teachers. She said, "A child coming to school hungry has behavior problems. They're all rude and crude. I don't know whether a man would have tried to find out what was wrong with the child." As these words suggest, getting to know the "whole" child was an integral part of segregated education, and it was a key to understanding the gendered component of how these women defined their work as teachers. The positive effects of a holistic approach to teaching children was something they had experienced in their own young lives, and they were keenly aware of doing the same for their own students. They knew no other way. The ethos of sharing, of "lifting as you climb," of combining the unpaid with paid labor inevitably infused how they approached their work.

This mission of uplift and preparing their own for survival was characteristic not only of teachers but of other professional women as well. Speaking specifically about her work in African American communities, a former social worker expressed that sentiment when she said, "I felt that we had a service to offer people, lifting people, motivating people, helping people to realize their own potential." Another social worker tells how she interceded with a White psychiatrist for a Black boy who suddenly found himself orphaned due to a car crash that killed his mother:

> And this boy's mother was killed and he was about thirteen. And the boy just sort of went off. So they had him down on psychiatry. So when we had our team meeting, the psychiatrist said, "Well, I don't know [what to do] with him; he's just acting so bad and everything." So I told him, "Look, I feel like you should let the boy join the human race. Everything he's had has been snatched away from him. At thirteen you wouldn't know what to do with yourself either but act up and be bad. So let him join the human race. He needs counseling, and he should be turned over to the Welfare Department [so that it] can find a good home, where there's a father and a mother. And tell them it's not going to be easy. But if they're dedicated people, I think he can be helped."

Her confrontation enabled a sad and confused boy to "join the human race" instead of being sent to a detention center as was the psychiatrist's initial intent. This narrative points to something else that is important. It illuminates how one woman's position as a professional can become a community asset. Her individual achievement symbolizes a group strategy for survival and resistance.

Finally, a family doctor with forty years' experience muses on her philosophy of medicine and how she approached her African American patients:

> Helping people was the key. People were depressed, in bad situations, [and] a big part [of my job] was listening. You treated a family. If the mother told you she had a headache and the day before her daughter was in [the office] pregnant, you knew the source of the headache.

Repeatedly we heard women speak about the importance of family, and we heard women use familial language to describe their work. These women, whatever their professions, approached the people or children they served holistically; they saw them as part of their racial family. They strove to pull them up and to facilitate their resistance and their chances of survival.

Gender Matters in African American Work Settings

Although racial and gender inequities were typically intertwined within the Black American work environment, Black women who found themselves in predominantly African American settings often discovered gender to be a more personally salient factor than race.[11] Our conversations with the thirty women (mostly educators) who worked in such environments support this notion. It is also clear, however, that retrospection heavily influenced the ways that most of these women recognized gender hierarchy and gender discrimination. Nevertheless, it seems that the gender inequities that had been invisible to them or taken for granted in other situations at younger ages—particularly within the context of primary groups and informal relationships—became more striking within formal groups and secondary relationships. Recognizing the ramifications of working daily in an environment where men were the majority is key to understanding these women's experiences. For instance, the minority who claimed never to have experienced gender discrimination were those who worked in predominantly African American female environments. Even in those settings, however, there was no guarantee that gender discrimination would not take its toll. A nurse, for example, remembers what it was like for her supervisor, the chief nurse, to meet with male doctors: "When our [female] chief nurse came out of meetings [with the medical directors], she would say, 'God, I feel like I [have] been cut with little razor blades all over.'"

Those who were most impassioned about the effects of gender discrimination, however, were the women who worked as professors and administrators in African American, male-dominated universities and colleges. We heard them repeatedly speak of being overworked, underpaid, and inadequately appreciated by the male administrators with whom they worked. For women who had gone to extraordinary lengths to acquire doctoral degrees that placed them among the academy's elite, their second-class citizenship among members of their own race often proved galling. Again, they spoke about the gendered nature of the commitment to race uplift work. Although all Black, middle-class Americans were expected to work for the betterment of the race, it is clear that the consequences of this commitment were different for women. Patriarchy shaped the different expectations and ensured that women's contributions had to be infused with deference to men and with an even greater level of personal sacrifice than was expected of male colleagues. Indeed, women told stories that illustrated that women's commitment to race uplift was often used in pernicious ways by male superiors in order to keep them in subordinate positions and to discourage them from complaining too much or too publicly about such inequities. They were "cooled out" by male colleagues and bosses; they were expected to defer to men's needs and ambitions. For example, one retired university professor who chaired her department for many years and directed her division for several more spoke of having experienced ongoing gender discrimination. Fighting against it was taboo—so much so that she "internalized a lot and got an ulcer." In discussing her career, she said:

[I was discriminated against as a woman] in pay, in promotions. [There was also] a double standard for evaluating my performance. One of my female associates studied the differences between women and men and was chastised. When I became Director I got $3,000 to bring me to the *base* for administrators at that rank. My contributions were not given equal evaluation or recognition as men. Evaluation(s) determined raises and promotions. If I made a speech or attended meetings or held [professional] offices, I was not given the same credit. I got a "3" and men got a "4."

This woman went on to tell how she always taught fifteen hours per semester in addition to the workload required by her administrative duties. As a result of her heavy workload, she experienced a further drawback that was mentioned by several other women professors—"lack of opportunity to do research or write." Retired women professors spoke, too, of the "academic perks," such as summer support, that were routinely given to male colleagues but not to them.

Despite the fact that most of the women held doctoral degrees, those who held positions in university administration usually worked most of their careers as administrative assistants, a title that, in the words of one, carried "the connotation in discussion with others . . . [that you were] secretarial and not administrative at all. Although [the latter] was the kind of work that you were doing." Promotions or opportunities to move up the administrative ladder were routinely blocked for women. One retired administrator bitterly complained, "When openings came, a second-rate man would be considered rather than the first-rate [woman] who knew what was going on." And then when "second-rate" men got the promotions, "[they] would have to come to you anyway for the information." Another woman remembers her blocked aspirations:

Several times there were openings in key central administrative positions, and I indicated an interest in them, and it was quite obvious that I was capable of doing the job. And the answer that I got was that it was a man's job and not a woman's job. I think it was a

gender problem. That, plus the fact that I'm not too sure that they
wanted to lose me from the position that I held.

As this comment suggests, she felt that because she was a woman
there was an underlying assumption that she should sacrifice her
individual ambition to the common good. Another story from a
woman who was well qualified to assume a major university administrative post reinforces how women were blocked for promotions and expected to accept this limitation. Of the university
in consideration, she said, "[It] is not good to women; [it] historically has not had women in top administrative positions."
Her words highlight how survival also dictated that these
women "pick their battles":

> And then a new director was hired, a male with less education, less
> experience [than I had], and I reacted, I objected. And the president
> of the university was adamant that he wasn't going to let me tell him
> what to do, that he was going to hire the man. Now this is when I re-
> ally ran into the sexism thing.

Here we see patriarchy at work, and we learn what happened to
a woman who was willing to test its strength. She faced a powerful and adamant man who was president, and her resistance
could only go so far. Ultimately, deference to male authority defined her survival. She, like so many other women in similar circumstances, tolerated such injustices not only because "this is
the way things were" but also because of their commitment to
helping "their people." To quit would mean giving up on service
to the Black community. Unstated but understood by these
women was the fact that their Black male supervisors knew this
and took advantage of it.

Women who worked in the mostly female world of elementary or middle schools gave accounts that suggest that they were
not touched as frequently by gender inequities. Nevertheless,
such environments were not without tensions between women
teachers and the few men who were almost always their principals. A retired elementary teacher was very pointed in her criticism of her male principals. She summed them up succinctly as

"jack-assed principals!" In the few cases where women were principals, they still felt challenged because they were women. The words of a former elementary school principal illustrate this:

> I remember that just because I was a female, as a principal people expected me not to be able to handle the situation—more because I was a woman than because I was Black. I guess that made me more determined that I was going to be good. I had people who came in the office and who assumed [that] I was the secretary, not the principal. You know, women weren't principals.

Those women who remained in the classroom throughout their careers often felt that they themselves would have made excellent principals, but in most cases they did not even apply for such positions. They were satisfied with the contribution they were making in the classroom, and they spoke of recognizing that their contributions directly helped improve Black children's lives and opportunities. One woman, in supporting her choice to remain in the classroom, said, "I was satisfied with who I was and what I did." Overall, they were keenly aware that administrative positions were largely reserved for men. As another woman summarized it, "Had I been a man, in earlier years, perhaps I might have moved into [the] principalship—I probably would have."

Not surprisingly, those women who taught at the high school level, where the number of men teachers increased considerably, were generally more aware of gender inequities. A former high school coach and chair of the physical education department recalled how shortly after integration she helped organize Black and White women coaches in her region to file a class-action suit for sex discrimination. In words that illustrate how the demise of segregation allowed at least some women to move beyond survival and to resist legally the inequities that all women faced, she explained, "We felt we were underpaid, and we really felt that we were doing more work than the men. And we felt that we just weren't being treated fairly." She went on to recount how some of the women in other districts "were threatened by their superintendents, and they were given $500 for coaching several activities, so they stayed out of it." "But we plowed on" was how she described the fight that led to the eventual law suit that improved the treatment of all women coaches.

Beyond the personal indignity of being denied positions because of their gender, of having to help less-qualified men figure out how to do their jobs, of enduring the endless games of deference to male colleagues and bosses, there was also a more critical inequity faced by all these women, one that continues to haunt them. Salary discrimination and lack of promotions seriously affected their incomes and, after retirement, their pensions. One woman with a doctorate from Columbia University who retired after twenty-eight years in a series of administrative positions at a university where "they gave men higher salaries for the same position"[12] "never reached $30,000, so [my] pension is small. The pension is unusually small because I never made any money."

Working with Whites during Legal Segregation

In contrast to the majority whose daily employment in a largely African American world offered protection from many of the personal cruelties of racial discrimination, there were those who worked in a predominantly White world prior to the 1960s. There they were openly treated as second-class citizens. A retired nurse remembers that when she started her nurse's training in 1949, "nursing was rough." While her training program was racially segregated, her practical experience was in a White hospital in which she was later employed. She spoke of what it was like to train and work in a hospital where "we were called names by the doctors and everyone else. They thought of us as dummies [and] gave us a lot of dirty work to do. The doctors called us maids [and] so did the interns." These doctors were probably arrogant to White nurses as well, but there is a distinctly racial component in their responses to the Black nurses. Clearly, not only did they assume that all Black American women were "maids," but their reactions strongly indicated that they believed intelligence was race-, as well as gender-, specific.

Insult was added to injury for some women in integrated settings when they had to take jobs well below their qualifications in order to survive. Despite considerable academic success that earned her a college scholarship, a retired government employee remembers why she did not go into teaching as she had planned:

> Well, I prepared to be a teacher. I got my undergraduate degree in education. It was during the time of segregation, so I had talked to someone who was going to be hiring for Tubman [middle school]. And they had told me that, yes, they would need me and that I would have a job there. And [they] had told me what the salary was going to be, which was $2,750 a year. And I happened to see an announcement on the bulletin board at the post office that Fort Mc-Donald was recruiting for clerk-stenos, and they were going to pay more than that for clerk-stenos.

She continues:

> I never should've been a clerk-steno with a degree in education. They hired lots and lots of [White] education specialists which were professional positions that paid a lot more. And somebody should've said to me, "Why are you applying for a clerk-steno, with a degree in education? We need you as an education specialist." Nobody ever said that, and it was several years before I found out about those jobs.

Another woman describes what life was like for her as a Black woman working with Whites in a blue-collar job prior to the 1960s. Although she retired from teaching, she started her work life as a seamstress for the army. She recalled, "We rode to work in the trucks that picked up the clothing. And we were discriminated against because the White women sat up on the front seat, and we had to sit back where they hung the clothing." She also remembered a detail that underscores how gender added a level of discrimination beyond race. She recalled that her male cousin who did the same work "made more money than I did." However, in a way that highlights the salience of race over gender in explanations of discrimination, this woman remained silent for a time when asked whether maybe both race and gender played a part in her unfair treatment. She finally responded, "I think it was because I was Black. And maybe it was because I was a woman, I don't know." Her description does not deny the possibility of gender's negative influence, but her words illustrate the overwhelming salience of race in her own mind.

Still another story illustrates how racism played itself out in the daily lives of those who worked in a predominantly White environment. A social worker talked about her experience as the first African American casework supervisor of a large city juvenile and domestic court. "I was not allowed to supervise White workers. They were [also] all men, and I don't think they were interested in coming to a Black woman." Although she gave this as an example of racial discrimination, her words imply the taken-for-granted nature of not just White but also male power. Without such privilege, there could have been no debate about her authority or the men's acquiescence to it. Yet, because they were White and because they were White men, they had a choice about whether to treat her as their superior.

Salary discrimination was, of course, a routine fact of life for those who worked among White colleagues. Another social worker recalled how she found out that she had been underpaid for four years. She discovered this inequity in the process of resigning to take another job:

> When I was dealing with personnel and I was getting all my paperwork done, the lady said, "My God! This is unfair." She said, "You came here as a master's degree social worker with experience in welfare, and they started you $5,000 beneath a woman [who] only had one year of graduate [school], and she was White."

These women also experienced blatant discrimination in matters of promotion, regardless of their geographic location. For example, a woman in elementary education in a Northern school told about her experiences as an African American woman in that setting. In the 1940s she applied for the position of acting vice principal in her school, but the job was given to a White woman. She confronted the White superintendent and asked him why she had not been appointed. "Is it because I'm colored?" After a long silence, he responded, "Well, it could be." Reinforcing her sense of injustice, the White woman who was appointed later commented, "Alice, let me tell you something. The only reason you didn't get this job is because you're colored. I'm telling you now. That's the only reason."

Sometimes the discrimination faced by these women was palpable, as we see in the case of a woman who worked all of her life for the federal government and eventually rose to a very senior position where she supervised personnel activities in more than twenty federal installations. (This is the same woman who planned to be a teacher but began full-time paid employment as a clerk-stenographer for the federal government.) She described the roadblocks she faced along the way because of her race. She remembered taking and passing a federal examination intended to allow her advancement:

> So anyway, I had already taken that test and made a 94. And I brought them the paper that I received with my score. And they said, "Well, this is too old; it's over ninety days. You'll have to take it again." I said, "Well, fine. I'll take it again." So they scheduled the test and all the applicants for this position had to take the test— about thirty-five people. I was the only one that passed the test. You'd think I would've gotten the job. I was not given the job. So, I always felt that was discriminatory. [But] that was before the civil rights laws were passed and before there was any avenue for lodging a complaint of discrimination, so I didn't say anything.

A few years later, she applied for another promotion and was turned down again. In her interview she was asked whether she had earned a master's degree since she joined the organization. (At this point, she had not.) She remembers the line of questioning that the male interviewer pursued:

> He says, "What have you been doing all this time?" And I said,
> "Well, I have been married, taking care of a home. I have had two
> children, and I have been working full-time all that time. So that is
> what I have been doing." And he said, "Well, you should've also been
> going to school. You could go at night." [Laughs]

Despite the clearly gendered nature of this conversation, gender discrimination was largely invisible to her at the time. She told the interviewer that "[he] was looking for an excuse not to hire me because I was Black. It never entered my mind that it might have anything to do with being female."

Even though women often resisted obvious acts of discrimination by speaking up and letting their awareness of injustice be known, their need to survive meant that they usually had to swallow their pride and go on to the next, perhaps more important battle. For example, the social worker who had lost four years of a significantly higher salary[13] summed up a common sentiment: "I guess I was just so tired of fighting at that time. I really should have challenged the city on that. But, I guess after you go through so many battles [laughs], you get tired of fighting." What was not said, but what the reader should know, is that this same woman had a long and venerable history of civil rights work at this point in her life. Prior to this incident, she had been involved in fighting bigger battles. She had worked with Martin Luther King, Jr., on several occasions, and, in her own words, she knew what it was like to have "the dogs and the hose loose on you." She had even gone to jail to fight for justice. Her comments take on a different meaning once we put them in the larger context of her own biography. With so many battles to be fought, she made a conscious decision that the matter of personal salary would not be one of them.

We end this section by examining the case of the one woman who worked in a predominantly White world but claimed to have had no experiences with racial discrimination. Because her case is unique, it allows us to develop a clearer understanding of the structural constraints faced by others. Indeed, her case provides a benchmark against which we can compare and contrast the experiences of others. Several dimensions of her work biography are worth our attention. First, she is the only one who spent the vast majority of her work life self-employed in the private sector of the economy. Thus, she had much more control over her environment than did any of the other women. Not only was she self-employed, but she also owned her own company, which often employed as many as sixty workers. Her business provided a luxury service to an exclusively White, elite, and wealthy clientele. Indeed, to be one of her clients suggested to the outside world that the client "had arrived" and could be considered part of the city's elite. Her hard-earned reputation allowed her to choose her patrons. Because they desired her services, it is likely that they were very solicitous of her. This level of control over her work life allowed her to stand in stark contrast to the other women and may help explain why she is the only woman in this group to claim that she never experienced racial discrimination in the workplace.

However, there is another critical factor that is important in helping us understand why this woman's experiences are so atypical. As a Black American woman who was a service provider (no matter how exclusive the service), she did not represent a threat to traditional race relations. In a very real sense, she worked behind the scenes. Her position was, in the minds of White clients, "backstage."

Although she also claimed never to have experienced sex discrimination in the workplace, her assertion is contradicted by her own descriptions of the challenges she faced as the woman in charge. For example, she used the following words to describe her relationship with her male employees: "I was sort of [the] head of everything." The choice of the words ambivalent "sort of" makes sense when she continues to explain that her husband worked with her in the business and that her male employees "would just try to ignore me. I think a lot of times, you know, they didn't respect me as a woman. [They] thought I shouldn't be [in charge]." Through reminiscences such as these, we come to appreciate how even the one woman whose work situation allowed for significant autonomy and independence still faced discrimination because she happened to be a woman.

Integration and the Elusiveness of Equality

Even with the arrival of legal integration, race continued to have significance in the work experiences of the women. Again, we examine education because it was within that institution that the majority of the women were employed—specifically in elementary and secondary education.

Teachers, whatever their race, confronted a new order of daily business as a result of the government mandate to integrate public schools. Legal integration forced the creation of a new system to replace what had previously been two separate school systems, separate professional meetings for the races, and different pay scales for Black and White teachers. What White teachers had always taken for granted was now extended to many Black American teachers. Suddenly, they found themselves with new books and available school supplies. They no longer had to use their own money to get their students the basic necessities. A former teacher who remembered, "I never had a brand new book," contrasts the situation after desegregation, where "Most of the time, if I asked [the principal] for something, I got it that evening or the next morning. Scared me so bad, I didn't know what in the world to do!" [Laughs]

Other obvious material advantages surrounded the dismantling of legal racism, such as better pay and better facilities, but desegregation also brought in its wake a variety of less positive consequences. Many of these women who had lived and worked in a predominantly Black world now faced the challenges that accompanied being in a work environment where they were not the majority. A former teacher described the earliest days of desegregation in her school, where 70 percent of the teachers were White. She recalled how important it was that "we knew all the Black teachers" because "I think it helped tremendously." Already well known to each other because they came from close-knit communities, it was clear from the comments of these women that the bonds among them strengthened as they faced the challenges of desegregation together. When asked to talk about relationships with their new White colleagues, one woman described them in cautious and telling words: "I don't want to say that they were terrible." Such a comment suggests much that is left unsaid. This, plus the fact that she immediately shifted the conversation to a former principal who had tried hard to create a positive atmosphere, "to make the tone for the school," suggests that she wanted to avoid discussing something that was negative. Indeed, by shifting the conversation, she tried to put a positive face on what clearly had been a less than positive situation.

Other stories point to the fact that the post-1960s era did not herald the end of discrimination and unjust treatment for African American women. Discrimination simply assumed different forms. In fact, a former guidance counselor claimed that her troubles began with the arrival of integration. She said, "I didn't really experience [discrimination] until integration came. I really didn't. [But] when they integrated the schools, I was head of the guidance department, and they sent some [White] folk from across town and I was in charge of the department and they resented it. And they let me know it!" In this case, the arrival of legal equality between the races may have influenced the balance of racial power and challenged the hierarchical nature of White privilege, but it didn't stop Whites who now had to report to a Black woman from registering their disapproval of her authority. Time, however, sometimes made for improved relations between the races. For instance, when we asked this woman if things improved over time, her comment is a fair representation of what several other women said: "It did. They [Whites] respected me for who I was. They realized I was devoted to what I had to do."

What these women educators learned about working in desegregated schools was that race took on a significance different from its role during segregation. The dominance of race now appeared in new and different forms that required new and different strategies for survival and resistance. While the rules shifted and the players appeared to come to the table as equals, the game changed little for them. These women spoke vehemently about the price African Americans paid, and continue to pay, to be part of a system where equality remains largely elusive. They recalled at length what they saw as contradictions of a system that was meant to improve the condition of African American life but that nonetheless had so many negative consequences for them. As Black American educators, they found themselves the targets of new forms of discrimination. For example, the closing of Black schools created employment hardships for many. Statistics from that era indicate that large numbers of Black teachers and principals lost their positions. A few simply quit, among them a former executive secretary to the principal of a large Black high school. She recalls that, "When I heard that integration was coming, [I took] the Federal civil service exam," and before long she was offered and accepted a ninety-day temporary job with the federal government. She still remembers the conversation she had with her astonished Black principal, who asked her, "Are you going to quit your job—your permanent job for a temporary, ninety-day [job]?" Her response provides insight into reasons that some abandoned the security and seniority of long-held jobs:

> I felt like if I go to a school and we integrate, [then] I would be the secretary who had to sharpen pencils. I knew that [that] was the way it was going be because I was Black, and [there was] no way I was going to get into that. So, I got out before they integrated.

Those who were hired by the White establishment faced other new challenges. Classroom teachers recalled how, in the beginning, some White parents "were very hard on Black teachers." One former teacher claimed that "White parents did not want their children taught by a Black teacher." Another explained it this way: "I think they were apprehensive simply because they had read [that] Black teachers were not as good as White teachers." Others remembered how some White parents not only did not respect Black teachers but "made [things] very difficult for them." A number of former teachers recalled how White parents routinely questioned any grade below a B, implying, as one former teacher put it, "that it was my fault because [their child didn't get an A." A former elementary teacher in a large Southern city talked about the pervasiveness of White racist attitudes. She spoke at length about the "poignancy of racism" she experienced from parents in the poor White neighborhoods in which she worked in the mid-1970s. Recalling a specific incident of racism, she said:

> I was teaching the Whites from Maryhill, and you are talking about some folk who are poor as Job's turkey, where incest is just rampant, where lice and filth is the order of the day. And I had this little boy who was in my class and, anyway, he had lice in his head. And the mother came to school and said, "Well, he got it from that old Black teacher that's teaching there." I made it a point to prove [that] Black folk are not the ones that really carry lice and filth and dirt. I went down to the public health department and got data to prove to her that Black folk are less inclined to get lice in their heads than Whites.

Apart from its blatant racism, this narrative demonstrates how race and class intersected to the disadvantage of the teacher who was formally in authority. It shows the assumed privilege that being White gave a lower-class mother and, in turn, the lack of privilege that accompanied this Black American middle-class teacher. By contrast, it seems inconceivable that a White teacher would ever be so accused or, if accused, would feel the obligation to defend her entire race from such an inappropriate slur. One can only imagine how difficult it was, after working in a system where the teacher's authority was nearly sacred in the eyes of the community, to find oneself in a situation where students and their parents often assumed that one was either unfair, less than competent, or unhygienic.

Sadly and with some anger, a number of retired teachers discussed an especially disturbing consequence of desegregation,
namely, the predicament of Black American children in the
newly desegregated schools. Desegregation created a new world
where these children were no longer surrounded by teachers
who knew them, knew their parents, and understood their communities. Although most Black teachers survived this separation,
many Black children did not. In a very real sense, desegregation
meant that Black teachers lost control of Black children, and
many of these women felt sure that, as a consequence, "something was lost." In fact, one woman forcefully told us that "we
lost ourselves. We lost our children." Rarely did these women
suggest that White teachers intentionally mistreated their Black
students. Instead, it was their uniform assessment that White
teachers did not understand Black children, that they lived in
what one woman called a "little antiseptic world" and hence
were ill equipped to teach Black children. The notion of teaching a subject rather than a child captures the essence of the difference these women saw in how White teachers approached
Black children. Social class also played a distinct role in this
judgment. All the women were clear that their own children,
those who were now among the most elite Black Americans,
managed to flourish in a desegregated system because their parents were able to provide them with the tools necessary for survival and resistance. Many spoke, however, of the devastating effects desegregated schools had on the "average" Black child.
Each had a different way of describing this effect, and, of course,
all recognized that the issue was an enormously complex one
that involved many factors. Two lengthy quotes paint for us a
picture of why these women see the White world and White
teachers as problematic. In the second narrative we hear the
longing for a return, not to inequality, but to the shared sense of
mission that characterized Black segregated education:

> I think with integration, with White teachers, I think [that] they're
> sincere, I really do. But I think they come with certain myths. One

of these is that [Black children] cannot learn, or they can only learn so much. And this is the way they operate. This is just from where they have grown up. They are in their own little White world. They are not going to live next to any Black people, they're not going to know any. All they do is read a magazine, or read a book, and it's a subjective thing. It's not objective. It's very sub- jective. Well, that's what they grew up with all around [them]. Then, when they get in a room full of little Black children, you know all of these things come to play. And they really don't know what to do.

Oh, if I could turn back the clock, I would segregate the schools again, and I would get all of those good, fine Black teachers. And I'd get them in and they'd work for our youth. Because when they worked with them, they got respect. Kids respected them. I think this is what happened to the schools. We have now an integrated school system where there have been Whites who have felt that [Black kids] are not going to learn, they're hoodlums, so that's what they expect, and that's what they get.

While most women tempered their criticism of White teach- ers, one former educator, a woman who taught for more than forty years in elementary school and who is still very active as a community leader, was less charitable. Indeed, she was adamant that, both in the classroom and beyond, Whites in general did not try to understand Black people. "Accommodation and un- derstanding have always been one-way," she argued. As her words make clear, she wanted to register the taken-for-granted nature of the White privilege that accrued to the researcher's race: "We've had to understand you. We've had to figure out your world and what made you tick as White people, but you've never done that for us. You've never tried to figure out what is special about us, what is our uniqueness." Her message is that Black Americans are by necessity bicultural. Their survival has been predicated on understanding, "figuring out," the dominant culture. By contrast, she argued, Whites as the majority group have not made an effort to understand or appreciate African Americans.

Although negative encounters with White administrators and teachers clearly outweighed positive ones, some women also made reference to Whites who made things better, who treated all their colleagues as equals, who went the extra mile, who became friends. Overall, we sensed, however, that such stories were highlighted because they stood out in some way as notable, as exceptions. It is also our sense that these conversations, more than any others in our times together, were ones very much influenced by the racial differences between researcher and retiree. The women we interviewed dug deep to find positive examples of White behavior because they did not want us to think they were being unfair. Yet, as they spoke, they inevitably returned to how difficult things had been for them because they were African Americans. Perhaps one former teacher, who spent most of her life in segregated schools, summed up what others repeatedly implied about the more subtle aspects of racism that they encountered each day. She recalled how in her integrated school, "One of the administrators was very obviously a person who had trouble dealing with Blacks. And even though he tried to hide the fact, it eventually came out. Not verbally, but—it usually does [come out]. They can't hide it but so long."

As already suggested, some African American women who worked in a largely White work world found that opportunities opened up for them after the mid-1960s. This was especially true in the case of several women in our study who were able to take advantage of a predominantly White work world that now felt legal pressure to diversify its workforce and to hire and to promote women of color. Two cases illustrate how some of these women benefited from this shift. A woman who earlier had been denied a job as acting vice principal was able to leverage to her benefit federal affirmative action programs that forced employers to "go outside the mainstream." Her ascent in the occupational hierarchy began with a federally funded program that provided her with the opportunity to teach in a college for a year as a teacher-lecturer and field supervisor for student teaching. She then returned to her home base and "just started climbing faster and faster." How far and how fast did she climb? Returning to school, "I became what you call a project coordinator—that was a federal job but still in the school. Then the following year, I became a teacher to assist the principal. The following year, I became the vice principal. And the following year, I became a principal."

In another case a social worker described a similar opportunity structure. Over the span of her career, she held many senior positions as director of various programs and agencies in northern states. Finally, close to retirement, she moved South as a full professor in a southern university. In contrast to the assessment of almost all other women interviewed, this retiree suggested that being a Black woman had given her advantages that women or men of other races did not have. Her argument and her experiences highlight how personal biography is a factor in each woman's work history. For example, she made the point that Whites who held positions similar to those she held usually "were required to have higher credentials than myself; in other words [they were required] to have the doctorate, while I have held the same positions that they have held with a master's degree." In this regard, her story is different from those of the women who argued that they had to have more credentials and be better qualified than Whites in order to get jobs.

The Continuing Significance of Race and Gender

We began this chapter by looking at the forty-seven women who began their careers in the decades prior to the 1960s, but there are three women who began their careers later. We argue that the decade of the 1960s was a watershed that divided these two groups. During that decade, both the civil rights and the women's liberation movements created significant changes for both African Americans and women. The government became actively involved in ensuring fairer treatment for both groups in the world of work and in general. During this period, African

Americans and women not only became more aware of race and gender issues but became more vocal about discrimination as well. Still, what the comments and experiences of these women convey is that race and gender remained crucial to their social location.

The work histories of the three women who began their careers in the 1960s reveal differences between them and the women who started their work lives in prior decades, when race and gender oppression were so blatant. In our examination of the careers of women who worked in mostly White work environments, we showed that the post-1960s era provided new opportunities for advancement for some. The stories of these three women lend credence to that observation. Unlike the women who started work earlier, they faced fewer structural constraints, because the most blatant forms of economic oppression of minorities had been reduced.[14] For instance, these women made no mention of blocked promotions and salary inequities. One of the women worked as an attendance officer in a predominantly Black school system, and she spoke of how "I felt like I received the promotions, quite, quite rapidly." Nevertheless, she remembered vividly the male resistance to her authority. The men she supervised, both Black and White, constantly challenged her authority. She said, "Sometimes it was out in the open, but most of the time it was kind of subtle."

Another, a former middle school principal in a predominantly White school, moved from teaching middle school through a series of other educational positions in fairly rapid succession and claimed that "I kind of think being Black has worked as an advantage for me, especially with integration, because they needed Blacks. I don't think my blackness worked against me." Her choice of words hints at the different world that these African American women experienced. In contrast to the older cohort, which experienced clear disadvantages based on race and gender, this younger group faced different career prospects. Now, White organizations "needed Blacks." To be a Black American ceased to be an absolute negative and, instead, sometimes became a qualified positive. As this woman spoke of this advantage, however, there was vacillation in her description. She began with "I kind of think" before continuing with the sentiment that being Black did not work against her. Further remarks reveal her awareness of the importance of gender. Recalling her decision to accept the principalship, she said, "When the superintendent asked me about taking a principalship, I really loved the school I was in and I didn't want to do that. And then I thought, if I don't go where they ask me to, then I won't open up room for another female." She also spoke of the difficulties she faced because of the perception that "women weren't principals." She felt that "it was more of a gender thing than a Black thing." Her words tell us what it felt like to be a woman in charge:

> I feel that everywhere I went I had to prove myself. I had to work very hard to show that I was competent, to show that I could do the job, to show that I could handle stress. Because when things go wrong, people look to see if you're going to cry because you're a woman, if you're going to fold up because you're a woman. And there were many times when I was in my office and I probably wanted to cry, but when I came out, nobody knew it. [Laughs]

As well as the obvious gendered component to this narrative, there is also a racial component. In fact, these negative experiences were likely a reflection of how race and gender in combination created discriminatory consequences.

The third woman who began her career in the 1960s occupied a senior position in state government. She was the first African American and the first woman to reach that level of seniority in her particular branch of government. She was sensitive to the link between gender and career opportunities. Like the other two younger women, she was also more cognizant of the interactions of race and gender in their careers than were the older women. Her awareness of the continuing struggle faced by African American women is reflected in these comments:

> I felt that everything that I attempted, I got hit on the head or kicked in the pants or just flat knocked down! And I've always tried to strive

to be the best because I knew everybody was breathing down my throat because [I am] Black and female. They say you can't do it, it's not going to happen, you won't accomplish it.

As these words suggest, being African American and being a woman ensured that her experiences in the work world would not be easy, even if things were less difficult than they had been for the older women we interviewed. In this sense, all of these women experienced race and gender discrimination. What distinguishes the two groups is not the presence or absence of such discrimination but the extent or degree of discrimination.

Fighting Back

There may also be another, more subtle distinction between these two groups of women. With the end of racial segregation and the enactment of laws to address discrimination in the workplace, greater equality between the races was fostered. A climate began to develop that allowed African Americans and women to discuss discrimination more openly and to seek redress at least some of the time. An example was given by the woman who worked her way up the promotion ladder in state government. She had been subjected to a blatantly racist work environment for many years. Her story allows us to compare two different time periods and to see how she responded differently in each. Here is how she describes the racial atmosphere in the office in which she worked for six and a half years at the beginning of her career:

I was the only Black, except for the janitor, in the whole office complex [of two or three buildings]. They [Whites] would go for coffee, they had a ritual, and they would go for coffee at ten o'clock. [The offices] would clear out, including the secretaries. And I would be left there, and not one of them in my office complex invited me for coffee. A White guy finally broke down and asked me to come have coffee, and I refused. And when he walked out, I cried. Because, you know—[I] wasn't refusing him, [I] was refusing the attitude there in the complex.

This narrative shows the woman's pain and rejection and how survival in the early years of this woman's career meant not fighting and how resistance meant accepting loneliness. Years later, we hear a different reaction on her part. Here is her description of how she finally confronted her White coworkers in one of her last positions:

> Well, I'll tell you the exact words I said. The door was open to the conference room and I said, "I'm not going to take this shit anymore!" And they looked at me and my boss says, "This is a public building." And I said, "I'm sorry I blurted it out, but I'm still not going to take this shit anymore!" I had gotten tired of having ulcers, and I said I am not going to allow these White people to make me keep getting ulcers. I said, "I'm tired of it." My mother tells me to hold my tongue, [but] I've held my tongue until I'm killing myself.

As is suggested in this account, the woman felt that she had already paid too high a price for her silence by jeopardizing her health. Survival now demanded that she actively resist. She recalled how her outburst was not planned but emerged from years of pent-up anger and frustration at the racism she had been subjected to. Noteworthy also is the obvious silence, the words unspoken in this encounter. Both the speaker and her White coworkers seem to know what is involved in the "shit" that she refuses to take anymore. Race relations in this particular situation demanded a coded confrontation on the part of the victim. But, as she goes on to point out, even this form of confrontation led to her being punished by the Whites with whom she worked: "My coworkers wouldn't speak to me for two weeks. [They] would pass me and wouldn't even blurt my name. And I told them I wasn't going to take it, I didn't care what happened to me. I had gotten to the point where it didn't even bother me if I lost my job." This last comment suggests something else that is worth noting. Given her senior position, she undoubtedly had ample information about formal avenues of complaint; she knew that she had recourse through the existing laws. She knew that it was highly unlikely that she would lose her job because of this type of encounter. Yet, rational assessment aside, her words reveal a level of frustration, a sense of hopelessness, that makes it clear that formal avenues of complaint would give little consolation in her daily battle to be accepted as equal.

There is another interesting angle to her story. It concerns the allusion to the generational difference between her mother and herself. It is a gap that existed between Black Americans of these generations, whether female or male. As such, it highlights the importance of historical biography in understanding different responses to racist encounters. In the days of Jim Crow, survival for her mother's generation of women and men required that they not engage in any direct confrontation with Whites unless forced to. The price of such confrontation was too high. For younger women, who worked in a less blatantly racist era, the price of confrontation with Whites was lower, but still not eliminated. Her story reveals the continuing discrimination and the effects of a hostile workplace on the human psyche. This successful woman, who had battled her way to the top of her division, chose early retirement at the age of fifty-four in order to escape this inhospitable environment.

Devotion to work and to doing the very best job possible is an important motif in the work stories of these African American women. As we have seen throughout the chapter, such devotion was influenced by a variety of forces over which they had little control. Their work biographies reflect the power of race, class, and gender, as well as the influences of historical and sociocultural forces, such as legal segregation. Their choices of professions and careers, as well as their work experiences, were governed by these constraints. Over and over again, we hear in their narratives the themes of survival and resistance. While their stories illuminate multiple "stumbling blocks," they also allow us to appreciate the tenacity with which these women approached such impediments. Despite all the obstacles, they managed to build the necessary "stepping stones" to success. The lessons learned in earlier life—to be the best, to pick their battles, to have self-confidence—were ones that they called on in order to successfully navigate a lifetime of employment under trying conditions.

6

Free at Last
Surviving and Thriving in Retirement

My last day there—you know what I wrote on my calendar?
Freedom! And I called in Dr. Massey [the boss] and showed it
to him. I laughed. I showed it to my secretary. That's what it
[retirement] meant. Freedom. Freedom to make my own decisions, to travel, to be with my family, to do whatever I
wanted to do. If I didn't want to get up in the morning, I
didn't have to get up. Of course, that never happened because
I'm an active person. I get up early. I get going. But that's
what it meant to me. Freedom to be who I want to be and to
do what I want to do when and if I want to do it.

> (A curriculum specialist with a master's
> degree in special education)

This chapter brings us to the retirement years. After
they had put in so many decades of hard work and struggle, we
were gratified to hear the women say that life in retirement is
good. They told us what retirement means to them and about the
sense of freedom it brings. They told us about the financial and
social preparations they made and how those preparations and
plans are paying off. They spoke of their hopes and dreams for
the future and how they are tempered by their concerns and anx-
ieties about the present. We learned how these lives, so rich in
experiences, are now being shared with others, especially
younger generations, as these women quietly go about leaving
their legacies of survival and resistance. Their work in the

church, schools, and other community organizations leaves them little time to complain about growing old or to bemoan their personal losses. As they shared their accounts, we heard echoes of recurrent themes that have become a part of the fabric of their lives, and we noted again how their personal biographies are intimately linked to a particular social and historical context. And, of course, race, class, and gender remain today, as in the past, significant forces as their life stories continue to unfold.

Free at Last

The joy and satisfaction these women feel was apparent as we talked to them about their lives in retirement. The one word that kept being repeated as they spoke of what retirement meant to them was freedom—freedom from schedules set by others, freedom from the responsibilities of the work world, freedom to travel, freedom to play, freedom to sleep late, freedom to do what they feel is important to them. One woman summarized the meaning of retirement this way: "Retirement means *freedom*. Freedom to do whatever you feel like, whatever you can get the energy to do. [laughs] Freedom to go to lunch when you want to; to go to the movies as often and as long as you want to; to go to meetings if you feel like it; to read as much and as late as you want to; to just enjoy your friends. No restrictions."

We cannot be sure to what extent the choice of the word "freedom" to describe the meaning of retirement is typical of other categories of retirees. What we know is that in terms of these fifty women's work lives, it makes a great deal of sense. They never felt that they had the freedom to choose whether to work. They went to work, in most cases when they were quite young, to help supplement family income or because their parents thought it was good for them or because it provided opportunities for them to be with their parents, especially their mothers.[1] They entered the work force full time as soon as their educations were completed, and they remained there until retirement. Only a few women had the luxury of dropping out after the birth of their children and remaining in the household as full-time housewives and mothers. The low salaries paid to Black Americans and the precarious nature of most of their husbands' jobs in a White-dominated society precluded this as an option in most instances. One woman still regrets that she did not have the option of not working when her children were small. She lamented, "I wish I hadn't had to work as much as I have had to. I never had that choice. It's not that I'm bitter about it. I think it's just that I wanted it, and I didn't have it." For most, working even when their children were quite young was a matter of survival, not of choice. It was a survival lifestyle they had learned from their mothers and from earlier generations of Black women who had successfully combined mothering and working outside the home. It is little wonder that when at long last they were given the opportunity not to work, withdrawal from the workplace would be seen as freedom. Not since they were children had they been so free from the necessity to engage in paid labor. Nevertheless, even this coveted freedom is in some ways racialized. Later discussions will reveal that many of the activities that they choose to pursue in their free time are in part dictated by their sense of obligation and responsibility to their race.

Satisfaction with Retirement

Almost without exception, the women expressed enthusiastic satisfaction with their retirement years. In fact, only two voiced any dissatisfaction. In one case, a woman's neighborhood had declined with the intrusion of drug dealers and the exit of long-standing residents. In the other, a woman's husband had divorced her in later life, leaving her with unanticipated financial problems at a time when her health was just beginning to fail. Otherwise, we heard only favorable comments about this time in their lives away from full-time paid employment. A lifetime educator, married and still living with her husband, made some typical remarks: "I'm extremely satisfied with my life. I'm doing what I want to do, and things have been going pretty well. We're in reasonably good health, and we're able basically to get things that we want, you know. The children are grown up, and we can spend our money the way we want. We get up and go. We're going to a football game tomorrow, as a matter of fact, in the Meadowlands in New Jersey. So we'll be gone for the weekend. Things like that." Travel, in fact, is a favorite retirement activity for many, and travel takes most well beyond New Jersey. Cruises, especially in the Caribbean, seem to be very popular. Married women travel with their spouses, but single women find travel companions in siblings, close friends, or tour groups where they are matched with other singles. A retired professor and college administrator said, "I'm satisfied. I should say very satisfied, because I am. Very, very. I'm blessed to be able to do what I do, even though it's hectic. I don't have to run to the doctor. I don't have any aches or pains. I'm in pretty good health, [but] I can't say no. I just don't know how to say no [to offers to take on church and community involvement]. It's just a loyalty and commitment."

To say that these women are very happy and satisfied in retirement is not to say that they are totally free of problems and concerns. They experience the same irritations and stresses that dog many other people of comparable status. There are some who could use more money and a few who are plagued by annoying chronic medical conditions. Cars break down or won't start, and household appliances demand repair. They overextend themselves and find that they are serving on too many boards and are involved in too many community activities. Family members get ill, and spouses and friends become too demanding. They sometimes perceive conflicting demands on their loyalties and are forced to make difficult choices. Yet these conditions would exist whether they were retired or working, and retired is definitely better. Retirement itself is perceived as good and rewarding, and, generally, they would agree with the former teacher who exclaimed, "I just think it's [retirement] wonderful." But wonderful is probably not the word most retired African American women would use to describe their struggles for survival in their retirement years. How is it so for the women of this study? Once again, it must be pointed out that they do not fit the collective statistical profile of older Black Americans, especially old, Black women, a majority of whom are single and poor and many of whom are in poor health.[2] And while it is true that rich or poor, Black or White, most people make a satisfactory adjustment to retirement and report that they are indeed satisfied, it is also true that adjustment problems are concentrated among those who are poor, sick, and uneducated.[3] We feel that the obvious happiness these women enjoy in retirement is greatly enhanced by their good health, their financial security, and their involvement in personally meaningful activities.

Good Health

A majority of the women perceived themselves to be healthy. Forty-one judged their health to be either excellent or good, with about equal numbers in each category. The "excellent" responses were rarely qualified, and only occasionally would someone reply "good" and add a qualifier; one, for example, said, "I have some sinus, but everybody has that. Every now and then I have a bout with some arthritis." Only a handful had any kind of chronic condition that would interfere with their daily living.

Good health, of course, is not entirely a matter of luck. It is, to a large extent, dependent on access to quality medical care as determined by economic capacity. While most of these women did not grow up in families wealthy enough to provide regular pediatric care, they spent most of their work lives as professionals. Over the past several decades, they enjoyed employer-paid group health insurance. Today they have both ample money to pay deductibles and the good judgment to purchase supplementary health insurance.

In spite of their present healthy state, continued good health was mentioned by thirty of the fifty women when they were asked about their hopes for the next five to ten years, and at least half of them mentioned some aspect of physical decline when asked what they liked least about growing old. Typical statements made were "I hope I will continue to be as healthy and active as I am today," "I would just like to stay healthy," and "I hope I will continue in good health." They often expressed these sentiments in the same breath with the desire to maintain their independence. Frequently heard comments were "I think it's important for me to maintain my health as it is, and that way, I can be independent" and "My hope would be that I could remain reasonably healthy and to be as independent as possible for as long as possible." It was also interesting to note how often women mentioned the desire to remain healthy, not only so they could remain independent but so they could continue to serve others and the community. It was not unusual to hear "I hope I will continue in good health so that I can serve others" or "I hope for mental and physical health so as to continue to be in a position to continue to share with others."

A Comfortable Lifestyle

Along with good health, most of these women enjoyed better than average financial security. We had not been interviewing long before it became apparent that we were talking to a mostly affluent and privileged group of women. The homes they live in, the cars they drive, the clothes they wear, and the social activities they pursue all reflect a solid middle- to upper-middle-class lifestyle. Exceptions were few. Only thirteen women live on less than $2,000 per month, and eighteen have household incomes exceeding $3,500 per month.[4] Unlike the sporadic job histories of many African American women who are forced to work on the fringes of the economy, the careers of these women have allowed them years of continuous work in a chosen field. They spent most of their work lives in jobs that offered benefits, paid them enough to accumulate assets, and provided them with pensions. They are highly educated, professional women. In view of these facts, the surprise is not that their retirement incomes are so high but that they are so low. They are remarkable only because we are talking about Black American women. For Whites of comparable educational achievement, career backgrounds, and work histories, especially White men, these income statistics would be considered rock bottom. Even though these women entered the labor force as young women and remained continuously employed until they reached retirement age, thus maximizing their pensions, their salaries were lower than those of White men for most of their work lives. Speaking about racial discrimination in the job market, one woman exclaimed, "I know that there are many jobs that I could have gotten had I been White. I could have gotten better-paying jobs. I've never earned enough money. I've never earned the value of the job." Another woman, whose retirement income is $28,000 per year, pointed out that, given her job title and experience, her income would have been much higher had she been a White male. Now, in their old age, as in the rest of their lives, the women find that their rewards are reflective not just of achievement and merit but also of their race and gender.

Most of these women have adequate retirement incomes today not because of a lifetime of tremendously high professional salaries or because of inherited wealth but because of financial planning that began early in life. Over and over again we were told of financial plans for retirement. As a matter of fact, only four women said that they had not made special financial preparation beyond pensions and social security. Financial investments were often diversified and included some combination of savings, stocks and bonds, IRAs, annuities, and property. For example, one woman said that, in addition to her pension and social security, she had, "a small savings and a couple of CDs." Another said that she had "set up IRAs and invested in stocks and bonds."

Financial planning for most, however, was much more complete than just devising ways to increase monthly income. Other kinds of preparations were made. Home mortgages and automobile loans were paid off, credit card debts were reduced, major home repairs were completed, and budgets were reworked. A retired school teacher told how her financial plans for retirement included "investing some of my income, purchasing and paying for a piano and a dryer, and buying my last car and completing the house mortgage." Another woman, widowed before her retirement, said, "The last five years I participated in two IRA plans and increased the amount invested in my pension plan. I had a new roof put on the house and paid off the remaining mortgage. I also reduced, conscientiously, the amount owed department stores which had extended [me] credit. I had a financial adviser, a CPA, help me decide on the best plan to follow. So far, so good."

The kind of foresight in financial planning that these women showed is not common in our society. An earlier study of retired professional White women that we completed several years ago found financial preparation for retirement to be rather rare among them.[5] Although they, too, were well educated, they had not really planned for lifelong careers. Economic reversals in their families, especially with regard to the Depression of the 1930s, had necessitated that most of them work, at least until marriage. Certainly, they had not planned to remain in the labor force their entire lives. They were supposed to have gotten married and to have had husbands to take care of their financial futures. Consequently, most of them had not prepared financially for their retirement years beyond social security and whatever company pensions they might have accrued. The group of Black American women we studied, however, was different. The women started early in their lives thinking in terms of careers to take them out of poverty or to ensure a desirable level of living for themselves. They had been taught from the time they were little girls to depend on themselves, that, because of racial injustices, the men in their lives would probably not be in a position to provide financial security. This was just one of the lessons of survival and resistance that they, as Black American females growing up in a segregated, racist society, were taught by their families. They had witnessed firsthand how their parents had managed economic survival in a world of greatly restricted opportunities.[6] These lessons, absorbed in childhood, stayed with them throughout their work lives and are now proving their worth in their retirement years. Economic independence represented not only a survival strategy but also resistance in the face of a world that would have them believe that they would probably end up eking out a living working in a White man's kitchen or making his beds and rearing his children. Now that they are older and find themselves financially secure and satisfied in retirement, they feel blessed but not surprised. As one woman notes, "Things seem to have gone as I planned."

Involvement in Meaningful Activities

Planning for retirement went well beyond preparation for financial security. It also included plans for activities to fill up the days and to provide meaning in the remaining years. Some women made plans that reflected anticipated changes in lifestyle. Some mentioned the special care they took to cultivate closer relations with extended family members as retirement drew near. Others planned to take adult education classes and to travel, both in the United States and abroad. Many looked forward to greater participation in church and other religious activities. Most contemplated volunteer activities in the service of the community, specifically the African American community. Their plans and expectations are being fulfilled. They are staying busy; some say they are "busier than when working [for pay]."

Analysis of their many activities led us to divide them into two broad categories.[7] First, there are those activities that represent involvement, albeit more intense, in lifelong interests and pursuits, such as friendships and family relations, church work, and

organizational memberships including African American sororities. A retired social worker's statement of her retirement plans
epitomizes these types of maintenance activities. After explaining the development of her financial portfolio, she went on to
outline how she prepared for other aspects of her retirement life.
She said:

> I maintained active affiliation with civic, professional, community,
> and religious organizations. I cultivated friendships with young
> adults and family groups in addition to peers and professional asso-
> ciates. I pursued opportunities for cultural and recreational activities,
> including international and domestic travel. And finally, I maintained
> an active social life.

The second category of activities incorporates all those endeavors that seem to be shaped by their lives as African American women. This category includes activities that enable them,
as privileged Black women, to give back to their race. Such ven-
tures are not new to them. Certainly, teachers were involved in
racial uplift efforts most of their work lives. However, in retirement they must seek new outlets for this effort. The freedom that
retirement has brought allows them to pursue this interest vig-
orously and in ways not permitted during their hectic professional work lives. A retired federal employee summarized it this
way:

> If we achieve something, we have to give something back. We've al-
> ways known that. Everybody Black knows that. That's why you hear
> the basketball players and the football players that are making such
> a wad of money, always doing something- establishing some sort of
> foundation or working with the ghetto kids or doing something. Be-
> cause they know they have got to give something back. That's just—
> that's the creed in the Black community.

Of course, these two categories—activities that represent continuity and those that represent racial responsibilities—are not
mutually exclusive, but we think that making such a distinction
offers insight into their motivations to stay active as retirees.

CONTINUITY OF ACTIVITIES AND INTERESTS

Although activities and interactions were diverse, much of the satisfaction these women take in their retirement years comes from simple, everyday activities in and around the home and from the enhanced opportunities to interact with family and friends. A recently retired sixty-five-year-old childless widow who lives alone described the types of things that filled her days and brought her pleasure. She said, "Oh, I don't miss it [work]. No, I do not. I walk in the morning. I get up early and walk, and I water my flowers, and I do my things. I am enjoying doing some of the things in the home I wanted to do, because it's the first time I ever had a home and could enjoy it." She went on to say that she enjoyed doing things with her sister, who lives just blocks away. "Twice a week we go for swimming or water classes, as they call them. We go there together, including her husband. And we have planned an October trip back to Georgia and Alabama [to see relatives]. And we have planned a Christmas cruise to the Caribbean. We talk each day on the phone. She's sort of my confidante. She's my best friend." She is also developing new friendships. One is with a woman she has met on her daily walks. "It might work up to that [friendship] because this morning we started talking about some church things together. And we know some of the same people, so it might develop into something. Who knows?" Another sixty-five-year-old, married and living with her husband, described her busy retirement days in the following way:

> When I first retired, it meant having more personal time—not having to get up at 5 o'clock. It means not having so much stress in my life—having more quality time with activities that I enjoy—more quality time with my family. We have always been a family who traveled on the weekends because we wanted to provide exposure for our girls. That is why we had somebody in the home to take care of the cleaning. And my being a nutritionist, while I was working, I always planned a three-week cycle of menus, so cooking was not a problem if you have the menu. I planned a market list that matched the cycle.

Anybody could do the shopping. So while they were growing up, we always traveled. There is absolutely no place that they have not traveled in New York or Canada. You know, we've been just every place. So retirement to me means being able to sit down and to listen to my husband more often—for him to listen to me more often. Now, however, we seem not to have as much time, since our grandson occupies everybody's time. He's in full control. My mother keeps him on Mondays and Wednesdays at her apartment until I pick him up at noon. Then I bring him home, and we keep him here for the rest of the day. So it's a family matter. We are all just as busy as we can be, and he is simply just a sweetheart. But now because we are home Monday through Fridays, we are planning more getaways [on weekends]. We went away for the last two weekends. We have a time-share, so my husband and I left last Friday, and we came back Sunday night. We were away the weekend for a small getaway. We can't go far, because we have to get back on Monday to keep the baby. So we are going to do this sort of thing and take care of our grandson and nurture him.

These two women's descriptions of how they satisfactorily fill their days in retirement demonstrate not only their shared social class achievements but also some of the differences we observed between those who have children and grandchildren and those who do not, those who are living with a spouse and those who are living alone. Those with husbands and children and grandchildren spend more of their time in a tight circle of family and interact more with siblings, cousins, aunts, uncles, and nieces and nephews. This is not to say that they neglect friendship outside the family. For example, a sixty-six-year-old married woman living with her husband has two children and four grandchildren who live out of state. There are visits back and forth to see children and grandchildren and to sit with grandchildren when there is need or opportunity. She said, "We [she and husband] go out there and babysit. My daughter has a baby that's just turned seven months. She's gone back to work, and I've been going up there to babysit while her regular sitter is on vacation and that type of thing." However, she went on to say that she and her husband visit friends together and travel together. "We have basically the same friends. We play cards with couples, and we go out to dinner often. But I have some [friends] in my clubs that he knows but not all that well. I belong to a pinochle club and a bridge club. In fact, I am in two pinochle clubs. One meets in the day and one at night. I play cards about four times a month."

A married seventy-year-old woman has two children and two grandchildren living nearby and two children and three grandchildren living out-of-state. She is responsible for the care of her stepfather, who lives in a nursing home; she is also a member of a service club at church and is actively involved in a community race relations organization. Still, she said, "I see the children and grandchildren on a regular basis. We are very, very close—the family. That is what made my mother happy." She went on to say that she and her husband have mutual friends with whom they visit and go out, and yet she makes special time for herself. One of those times comes at breakfast, which might last one and a half to two hours. "Retirement," she said, "means a time that I can do some of the things that I longed to do when I was working, and the greatest one of those things is to have a leisurely breakfast. I really enjoy that. My children know that I do not want to be disturbed at breakfast. If they should call, and I'm having my breakfast, they say, "Oh, I'm sorry, mother; I'll call you back.""

Those who are widowed, divorced, or separated but who have children and grandchildren usually perceived the immediate family as the center of their social lives also, especially if those family members live close by. An eighty-one-year-old widowed business woman, mother of seven and grandmother of eighteen, retired nineteen years ago with her husband. They traveled extensively, taking four cruises and making trips to California, Hawaii, Florida, Spain, Africa, and "all the islands." Now she still "enjoys friends" and "visiting the sick in nursing homes" and "doing the things you craved to do in life and never was able to do while working," but she finds a special joy in her rich full family life, which revolves around her children and grandchildren. She said, "I enjoy, enjoy, enjoy the children, you know, and there are so many family things we can do together now. We have family reunions and things. They all like to come out here because I have lots of room." Five sons and fifteen grandchildren live in the area. All five sons have breakfast with her nearly every Sunday.

Fourteen women are childless. Those who are childless and married naturally do many things with their husbands, but they involve themselves with friends and extended family to a greater extent than do those with children and grandchildren. A childless, married sixty-five-year-old who obviously enjoys her home and husband travels with him and does "couples-type" things with him. But she and her two sisters also visit her mother and aunt in the nursing home practically every day. Her husband does not like basketball, which she does, so she travels with her sisters and sometimes her sister-in-law to tournaments without him. Of an upcoming tournament, she said, "I already have my hotel and my ticket and, you know, paid for my bus fare, and I'm ready to go. Already reserved my spot. I like that, being able to get away, to have enough time to go to things like that." She also belongs to a theater group and attends plays, ballets, and concerts regularly. If her husband is not available or is not interested, she goes with another family member or with a sorority sister. She also has nieces whom she likes to introduce to musical concerts and theatrical events.

Those who are single and childless, of course, are the ones most likely to find their social lives more exclusively revolving around extended family members and friends. A seventy-year-old single woman with one half sister, a stepsister, and two foster siblings who grew up in her father's household talked about family in broad terms. For example, she referred to her church as her second family and her sorority activities as another "family-type" thing. She sees and communicates with her sisters "periodically" and as often as possible on holidays and birthdays, and "then there are the cousins in New York." Another cousin lives in California. She had not seen her since she was five years old, but three years ago she established contact and now has made several trips to visit. "And there are male cousins in Brownsville with whom I am still close."

As women, the retirees in our study were particularly vulnerable to assuming the role of caregiver for older relatives. A number of them are now acting as the primary caregiver for a parent or parent-in-law or have done so in the recent past. This responsibility greatly restricts their activities and introduces new stresses into their lives. A sixty-four-year-old widow finds herself having to provide daily care for both of her aged parents. Her father is accustomed to being the patriarch and is finding his new dependent role difficult, which, of course, further complicates life for his caregiver daughter. Sadly, she explained her relationship with him:

> My father—well, I've had to take a stand with him. Because in his older age, he's very argumentative, and yells and screams and calls you names and all of that. Ummmm, I wish that were not so. It has gotten better. I went for some weekly counseling sessions and got to the point that I could say, "Now you're not going to talk to me that way," and could stay away. And that's what I really did. I think what got the message across was staying away from the house and not going. But I wish the relationship were different. My mother's relationship with me is—we've always been good friends, but she has got to please Daddy.

With few exceptions, then, we found that women were enjoying full social lives that involve family and friends. Black Americans, as Rose Gibson has noted, use informal network systems in meeting their needs. Whites do this, also, of course, but Gibson suggests that perhaps Blacks draw from a more varied pool, including family, friends, acquaintances, and church members, than do Whites in seeking their social supports.[8] Certainly, for these women, participation in such networks represents a lifelong tradition begun in their childhoods. At this point in their lives, they are happy to continue such relationships.

The community organization mentioned most frequently in terms of both membership and active involvement was the church. National surveys have revealed this to be true of older people in general. Studies also indicate that about 50 percent of older women have church membership, and about the same percentage attend church regularly, that is, twice a month or more.[9] The difference among these older African American women, however, is that their church memberships and involvement far exceed that of the older population at large. Ninety-eight percent of the women in this study belong to church, and 90 percent claimed to attend church at least four times per month. The explanation for this extensive church involvement, as well as for their involvement with family, friends, and neighbors, can doubtless be tied to the principle of continuity. The continuity principle teaches us that in making choices in life, people are attracted to coping strategies, ways of thinking, and people and organizations that have been helpful and supportive in the past.[10] Certainly the church would satisfy this standard for this group of women. The church has always played an important role in their lives, especially in their youthful and formative years. As we have already seen, the church was a major player in the survival of Black Americans in a racist, segregated society. In many ways it provided American Blacks the means of resisting the negative self-images the larger society would have imposed on them in its efforts to break their spirits and to destroy their wills. It is a very strong part of their personal identities, going all the way back to their childhoods. It remains a part of who they are today. Their personal comments support this point of view. One woman explained, "The church has been important ever since my childhood. It has been important to everything about my social, religious, and emotional development—to my self-confidence and family focus." Another woman, retired and with a master's degree in nursing, said, "The church was always the center of a Black person's life, and it still is [for me]: it's always been a very important part of my life." And still another voice confirmed, "The church is a part of my identity. It really, yeah, it truly is a part of my identity. I get my spiritual strength from the church, and I feel a sense of commitment." It appears, then, that the church is, as one woman put it simply, "a part of my being, and I take an active role in things there."

The church affords these women another opportunity to continue doing what they have always done, and that is to serve others. Most of the women were in service-oriented professions, and now they persist in those efforts through their churches. It was members of their church communities who offered them support and nurtured their self-confidence when they were young girls; it is only fitting, therefore, that the church has now become a conduit through which they in turn find opportunities to be of service to others. For example, a retired university administrator with a Ph.D. in social work from a northeastern university heads up her church's program for its older members. This program allows her to continue her professional interest in gerontology at the same time that she is working with a segment of the population that is important to her personally. As director of this program, she coordinates the efforts of one hundred fifty volunteers in her church who are matched with one hundred seniors. She is responsible for recruiting both the seniors and the volunteers who participate in the program, matching volunteers with older people and overseeing and planning many of the interactions that take place. She says, "I spend a lot of time up here with this project with my church, a lot of time."

It is interesting to note that even their service to others through the church is constrained by their past experiences and employment and by the fact that they are Black American women. As we discussed previously, these women were concentrated in the helping professions, such as social work, nursing, and teaching. Their unpaid work in the community as older women is an extension of the kinds of labor for which they were once paid professionals. Few of them spoke of serving on building and construction committees in the church or of taking part in financial planning or other business-oriented pursuits that are a part of church life.

In addition to the volunteer work they perform through their churches, these women donate countless hours of volunteer labor through a host of other organizations. Only one woman had no volunteer involvement in her life, but more than three-fourths reported participating in volunteer activities (other than the church) at least once per month, and half participated in such activities weekly or more. The list of affiliations includes golden age clubs, political and civic organizations, business and professional associations, Black historical societies, college alumnae boards, Black women's clubs, the YWCA, and senior citizens groups. Again, the unpaid services they render are often related to their paid labor during their preretirement days. For example, a former public school teacher, retired since 1978, participates in a local Kiwanis Club program and goes into schools to read to elementary grade children. The schools she visits are in the inner city, and the students are predominately African American. She explained, "I work with the young people. I go to Barton and Elkon school once a week and read stories to the children because I am trying to teach them the importance of knowing how to read."

A favorite association that the college-educated women have maintained down through the years is with their sororities. The two dominant ones, of course, are Alpha Kappa Alpha (Alpha) and Delta Sigma Theta (Delta).[11] Women spoke proudly of being an Alpha or a Delta, and one had even served as national president of her sorority. Again, these sorority memberships give their lives continuity and, at the same time, allow them the opportunity to serve others.

GIVING BACK TO THE AFRICAN AMERICAN COMMUNITY

In addition to the many activities already mentioned, the women participate in others that are almost purely racial in their orientation and that often represent new interests. These activities involve attempts to uplift and to advance the Black race. The undergirding motivation seems to be the feeling of obligation to give back to the race. As these women review their lives, they recognize that many people from the Black community helped transform their stumbling blocks into stepping stones. Now they feel it is their turn to do the same by doing for the next generation what was done for them. In this way, they make their contributions to the continuing struggle of survival and resistance that faces African Americans in our society. To be sure, "giving back," "uplifting," and "advancing the race" all involve service, just as many of the continuity activities do. However, these type of activities go beyond services that affect just individual lives; they influence Black institutions and support and foster values and patterns of behavior that the participants feel to be vital to the uplift of the race. For example, a retired educator with a degree in social work used her church connections to work with young African Americans. She recently coordinated her efforts with another woman at church in working with a group of teenagers, mostly thirteen and fourteen years of age. In describing the goal of their endeavor, she said, "We will be working with them in terms of their responsibilities as young people, responsibilities to themselves, responsibilities to their families, their church, their community, and this kind of thing. We are really implementing an educational-spiritual program that keeps them tied to basic family values, and that's something that's very important to me." It is obvious that this woman feels she is doing more than just serving a few Black teenagers; she believes she is giving something that will live on in the perpetuation of family values.

Consider another example, which has already been mentioned, of the former school teacher who now reads to elementary children as part of a Kiwanis Club program. In doing that, she is serving specific children, but it is apparent as she speaks that her objectives are much broader than just teaching reading. She said, "I read to them regularly, but I [also] talk on Black history or bring a part of my doll collection and explain to them where these dolls come from. Or [I] show slides of the various countries that I have visited, and I enjoy that." Obviously, in addition to reading, this woman is passing on Black history to the next generation. Her dedication to this project is exemplified by the fact that in one year she read to more than twelve hundred students, and she gave each one a book that she paid for with her own money. She had spent many hours searching used-book stores and discount stores in order to make this possible.

Uplift activities are focused on the youth of the community. Although different voices expressed it in different ways, they all spoke to the welfare of young people as the most pressing issue confronting the African American community today. Indeed, this is perceived as the very essence of the survival of the community and is of great concern to these women. Many spoke specifically of matters that affect youth, such as the prevalence of teen pregnancy and the increase in single parent households. Equally as worrisome are violence, crime, and the drug culture and the toll these problems are taking on young African American men. There is concern for the literal survival of an entire generation of men who will be lost if there is not a reversal of present trends. One woman seemed to speak for all when she said, "One of the biggest issues facing the Black community is the fact that the young Black male is seemingly being—what's the word I want to use?—just being annihilated. And they're doing it to each other. We seem to be losing a generation of young Black males. I don't know what it is that can be done about it, but something needs to be."

One thing is certain—these women are not going to leave the problems faced by disadvantaged African Americans entirely to someone else to address. They believe that they can make a contribution toward the younger generation's survival and resistance. Indeed, they feel obligated to do so. One woman summarized the prevailing attitude in these words:

> [We need] to identify and develop at the grass-roots level leaders who may have the potential, who will have the potential to give hope to our young. We can do it on an individual basis at work in

our various clubs, churches, and other organizations. We can do this as resourceful persons. We have to identify problems which do not allow for the enhancement of our people and to make progress in large numbers. See, most Black people have not arrived. We just circulate the same little groups as leaders. And those of us who are retiring, who are professional women, we are a tower of knowledge—of experiences of where we've come from, and what we've had. We must become a community of caring and reaching back, of caring and reaching back to help others pull themselves up by the bootstraps.

They feel that they have skills and knowledge that can be useful, and, now that they are retired, they have the time to focus their energies on helping Black youth. Part of what they do is done in a very personal way, that is, working one on one. Many would agree with the woman who said, "You can work individually. If you do something to help one child, if you help one child to stay in school and not get sidetracked and not have to take any job she can get but [rather] go on and finish school and get a good job, that's helping."

Some women work actively at mentoring. A retired public school administrator said, "I'm involved in a lot of things in the community and, yes, I think we do have an obligation to further the community—to share our talents, to give of our time and energy and our resources. I also feel that it's important for, especially for Black women, to help other younger Black women." She went on to say that it is important to mentor young women who are going into one's own profession. She declared, "I think it's important for us who have been in public school administration to mentor other females who want to do that. There are some things that they are doing that [are] going to be detrimental to their careers in the future, and I think that we need to do more in helping to guide them." Of mentoring, another woman said, "Older women need to become more aggressive in approaching younger [women] and offering help. Help needs to be applied to young parents before things go awry."

There are others who feel that they contribute just by the way they live their lives—by presenting themselves as role models. One woman said, "These particular young ladies at my church, I know they have a great deal of respect for me. And whatever they want to talk about, you know I'm there to listen. Oh, yes, I think it's our duty to be role models." Another echoed the same sentiment by saying that she made a contribution "just in the way I carry myself." Another woman, expressing her great concern for Black children, said, "I call them my kids, too, although I'm not married, and I don't have children. But I believe that we are all in a family together, and if our children are not prepared for the future, their failures will rebound on us. We'll lose, too. They're our future leaders, and they must be prepared to lead." She defends her choice to work only with Black children by saying, "I am not anti-White: I am just pro-Black. Because Blacks have been at the bottom of the totem pole, so to speak." She went on to say, "As I see it now, it's being mentors and finding ways to motivate young people to face challenges, to make them have a desire to discover who they are, and that they can do anything they want to do." This woman has found a very creative way to combine role modeling, mentoring, and community service. As the editor and proprietor of a small newspaper circulated in the African American community, she strives in her publication to present a positive image of Blacks to counteract the negative one so often portrayed by other media sources. She has solicited the assistance of twenty teenagers who write about the teen scene in the community. Each of these teenagers is matched with a mentor. She described her program and its objectives this way:

> I have twenty mentors who work with them on a one-to-one basis to help them direct their skills in a constructive or a productive channel. It's one thing to be good writers, but putting it to good use for a community expression is an extension of their creative skills. It also makes them conscious of the purpose or the need to be good at writing skills for any career option that they may select.

Those with young grandchildren often translated their concern for the youth of today into very specific concerns for their children's children. They lament that their grandchildren must grow up in a hostile world, a world that may lure them away from lofty and cherished educational achievements, a world that may, in fact, bring them physical harm. One grandmother had some difficulty in expressing her concern, but she put it this way:

> [I am concerned about] my grandchildren, and how they will be affected. I don't know how I want to put this—I want to say something about the way they're going to grow up, and whether they will be growing up. I'm really concerned about how they will get along in school, as far as, you know, the way they are being educated. And their school, that worries-that bothers me. They're getting along fine, but there are so many bad things happening in the schools.

Another widowed grandmother gets up at 5 A.M. each Monday morning and travels several hours through heavy traffic to take care of her grandson in another state. She spends the week and returns to her home Friday night. Sometimes she takes the train, but most of the time she drives. She admits that it makes life hectic for her, especially since she has a life of her own teaching an occasional college course, maintaining a home, serving on professional boards and committees, and staying involved in church work. Her daughter and her son-in-law are both busy professionals who can well afford expensive child care, but she believes that no one could do the job as well as she can and that a child in today's world needs the best there is. She summed it up by saying, "Yeah, yeah, he's worth it. You see, I know a lot about child care and a lot about children. I know that my daughter and son-in-law are very, very lucky, and I think [my grandson] is getting what he ought to have. It's too bad. Child care is the pits. Kids are in some awful situation these days."

While working with young people one on one is very rewarding for some, there are those who feel, because of personal talents or skills learned in their administrative positions, that a productive way to evoke positive change in the community and to advance the race is through organizational participation. One such woman said, "You can work with organizations where you have greater strength. I often go back to the saying 'In union there is strength.'" A former college administrator explained how she saw her role as a community activist. "I'm on boards and committees to try to see what can be done. I, you know, I write letters. I try to do position papers for different bills in the state legislature, and we hold workshops to help people understand and cope with problems." Still another woman who did not see her strength as "working in the trenches" saw herself making contributions through her membership and participation on various state-level boards and commissions. She said, "I view my contributions in the area of educating people about the problems. I don't go to halfway houses and things like that because it is not just something that I see myself doing. But I do get in the medium in which I feel comfortable."

This motivation to give back and to pass on a legacy to younger generations stems from a broad principle of obligation to their race, a principle instilled in them as small girls. These women were nurtured, mentored, supported and molded not just by their immediate family members but by citizens of their extended families and communities. They remember what church members, neighbors, and even strangers in the community did for them. This is behavior learned from the example of their earliest role models. What they are doing now just "comes naturally."

The great emphasis on sharing and giving back to younger generations seems intimately tied to the responses these women gave when asked what they liked best about being older women. Of course, there was variety, but the most frequently voiced advantage of being old had to do with the accumulation of experiences and the ensuing wisdom, which could now be passed on to the next generation. A retiree from the State Department of Health captured many others' sentiments when she said, "What I like best about being an older woman is the experiences—the rich experiences that I've had, and the wisdom that I've gathered along the way that I like to share whenever I can because I have had some very rich experiences." Another said, "I like the experiences from the past that help younger women. They lean on me a lot." The next most frequently liked aspect of being an older woman was being able to speak "one's mind," to "speak the truth without others taking offense." Comments like these, taken together, seem to indicate that what the women like best about being old is the fact that they have the wisdom of their experiences, which they can now share as a legacy with receptive younger generations. Perhaps this great concern with "giving back" and "passing on to others" also accounts for the notable absence of certain concerns about being old. Only one woman mentioned disliking what age had done to her physical appearance. Many gerontologists have written about the negative impact of loss of physical beauty or attractiveness on women in America.[12] This did not seem to be very important for these African American women. Perhaps those who continue to lead productive lives in their old age have less time to dwell on the changes that are taking place in their appearance. Feeling good about one's self on the inside may be enough to compensate for any loss of physical attractiveness that others may perceive.

Old Wounds Revisited

Even though the women's personal lives and those of their families seem secure in comparison to what they perceive happening to many African American youth in the community, the condition of race relations in the United States continues to haunt them. They spoke of bad race relations and community tensions, of societal apathy and the inhumanity present in the world today. They realize that their personal security, rooted in education and money, is not enough to protect them from the prejudice and discrimination that continue to plague our society. Some social scientists argue that old age has the attributes of a master status that overrides the significance of other statuses, including race. They assert that there is little evidence to indicate that minority groups suffer more degradation than their White counterparts of similar socioeconomic status.[13] Episodes from the lives of these women in retirement contradict such assertions. They are frequently reminded that, in spite of their socioeconomic standing in the community, they are often still judged on the basis of their race.[14] One account that illustrates this perception was given by a former college administrator and community activist who has a Ph.D. She recalled how shortly before the interview, while making a condolence call to the president of a board on which they both served, she was asked by Whites in attendance if she were the family's maid. Such reminders of how their lives are still configured by the intersection of race and gender not only are hurtful but indicate that the battle continues and that the armor of survival and resistance is still needed as we approach the twenty-first century.

We have looked at fifty older African American women who are happily retired and who are enjoying a lifestyle that many, especially other African American women, might envy. Many among them admit to being privileged. Still, the long arm of gender and racial victimization reaches from their past lives into the present. It is true that they are privileged, but not as much as they might have been had they been White and male. Given their educational achievements and their years in the labor force, they should be even more financially comfortable and secure than they are. Their lives of uninterrupted tenure as paid laborers are seen in part as a function of race and gender. Working for them was never an option; it was more a matter of necessity, a matter of survival. A lifelong emphasis on economic independence fostered unremitted planning, which they credit for the size of their retirement incomes, for their good health, and for their rich and full lives. Their lives are filled with a variety of activities that involve family and friends, but much of their time is spent in other arenas, such as church, school, and community. Working from the assumption that the fortunate should give back to the generations coming behind, they involve themselves in a great many actions of unpaid labor as they strive to lift the next generation. Perhaps this is the main reason that they do not seem to have experienced the loss of status that so often accompanies old age. These women epitomize the words on the Mary McLeod Bethune Memorial, in Washington, D.C. The words inscribed there at the foot of the sculpture capture the essence of what the women hope to leave to young Black people:

> I leave you love. I leave you hope. I leave you the challenge of developing confidence in one another. I leave you a thirst for education. I leave you respect for the use of power. I leave you faith. I leave you racial dignity. I leave you a desire to live harmoniously with your fellow man. I leave you, finally, a responsibility to our young people.

7

Pioneer Role Models

We began this book by arguing that the women in this study were pioneers whose lives command attention as models for present and future generations. We conclude by summarizing some of the ways in which this is true. In the pages that follow we briefly highlight what we see as the most compelling lessons of their life stories.

Early chapters illustrated the importance of family, community, church, and schools in their young lives. Although they occurred in the context of a legal system of racial segregation that was designed to denigrate and disenfranchise African Americans, these women's childhood stories reveal why the dominant group's efforts to break their spirits were so unsuccessful. Through their childhood recollections, we learn what it was like to grow up in a distinctly Black world where the key institutions of family, community, church, and school worked together to provide the tools the women needed to get ahead in life and to avoid being consumed by the inevitable racism they would face.

Although many of the women might characterize sexism as less virulent in its consequences than racism, patriarchy has also been a force to be reckoned with in their lives. In truth, the intersection of race and gendered systems of inequality created, and continues to create, a location for these African American women that places them at a disadvantage compared to similarly educated White men or, indeed, White women. Thus, their successes are particularly noteworthy because they were so hard earned and because they must be viewed through the prism of multiple jeopardies.

The women's adult work experiences illustrate the challenges and triumphs they faced in a lifetime of particularly trying labor force participation. Their stories provide inspiration for women and minorities today who continue to face various forms of oppression and discrimination. They can profit from the firsthand mobility tales of these African American women, most of whom grew up in poor or modest circumstances. Their persistence and resistance in the world of work should give hope to those who need reassurance that it is possible to survive tough challenges in the workplace.

Both women and men who anticipate their exit from the world of paid employment can profit from the retirement experiences of these women. Their lives in retirement are models that reinforce the extent to which positive aging is tied to being active and contributing members of the community. They help reframe our thinking about aging and specifically about what it means to be an old woman in this society. They stand in sharp contrast to the situations of so many old women in our society who feel unattractive and devalued. Despite the disadvantages of being old and female, these women show us that it is possible to reach maturity and old age and to still feel vibrant and good about one's self.

When we first met the women of our study, they had already reached maturity, and they had come to appreciate their successes and to feel good about themselves and their lives. The path to such a positive sense of self has been long and often difficult. The confluence of many factors helped to establish their patterns of achievement. For example, historical circumstances created a different form of gender asymmetry for African Americans than for Whites. Because African American men faced barriers that denied them access to the same employment and wage opportunities that White men enjoyed, African American women did not have the luxury of relying on men as their sole source of livelihood. Even if African Americans subscribed to the White society's "cult of domesticity" that relegated women to the home, a racialized economic reality denied them that choice. Instead, African American women learned very early in life the essential lessons of self-sufficiency and economic independence. Thus, lack of choice born from racist structures created a major strength in these women. They experienced "forced liberation" from a least some of the restrictions of conventional gendered norms.

Lessons from the Past

Current trends in the United States register women's increasing labor force participation and lifetimes of sustained employment. Fueled by changing gender prescriptions and by economic shifts that necessitate two-wage-earner families, a milieu has been created that stresses independence for women to an extent unknown in previous generations. This is especially true for White American women. Consequently, the future for most young girls and women in the United States, regardless of race or social class, is likely to resemble key dimensions of the life histories of the African American women in this study. Most women will enter the labor force and stay in it for most of their adult lives. Most will rear children while working both outside and inside the home. They will retire after decades of employment during which they will have established an economic base independent of that of the men in their lives. Finally, they will grow old in a society that views the aged, and especially old women, in an unfavorable light.

Although previously unrecognized as role models for Whites, these African American women have much to teach all women who are likely to travel this path of independence. While the structural barriers that impede gender and racial equity have been lowered, women and people of color still face discrimination.

Thus, many of the survival tools that stood these women in good stead may now have applicability for all women and minorities of today.

One of the most critical survival tools acquired by these women, of course, was education. From childhood on they learned its importance, and they learned the necessity of having educational credentials that would challenge employment systems that treated them as second class citizens. "If you're prepared, no one can take it away from you" was how one retiree remembered her mother's advice about the importance of education for Black American women. Another woman remembered not getting a promotion ostensibly because she did not have a master's degree. She recalled how this motivated her to get the degree by attending night classes for several years at a university in an adjoining town so that "no one could ever [again] say I didn't have the appropriate credentials for any job." Education was a passport not only to job security and a better paying job but also to a better life. Consequently, it is no surprise that all but one of the women in this study graduated from college and thirty-three out of fifty earned at least a master's degree over their lifetimes. Even though supported by spouses, friends, colleagues, and family members, they made considerable personal sacrifices to gain these credentials. For example, not all began their work lives as professionals with terminal degrees. A number of them left spouses and children over extended periods of time (typically during the summer months for teachers) in order to complete their education, and many denied themselves vacations and other pleasures as they worked to acquire these credentials. Sometimes it took years of sacrifice, but they were determined to finish their degrees. Certainly, those who were married with children would have much preferred not to leave their families. Most recalled how unhappy they were to leave behind young infants and children and spouses. Becoming "sojourner" mothers was clearly done out of necessity and not by choice. Like their mothers before them, they were forced by circumstances to become pragmatists and to take a long-term perspective. They had learned that "sacrifice on everyone's part today would lead to a better life for all in the future."

Networking became another tool of survival. We were both struck by the extent to which these women over their lifetimes developed impressive networks of similarly situated African American women. Through their varied group affiliations, they have accumulated numerous longtime friends and associates who have faced many of the same challenges. Together, they have created a powerful sisterhood that allows for the sharing of joy and sorrow, hope and pain. Almost all of the women we interviewed mentioned the importance of women friends. Many made comments like "my friends are very important." A seventy-six-year-old retired physician talked at length about her "five women friends who are very important in different ways." One of them has been a friend since kindergarden. She referred to her friends as "my support group," and she insisted that "they sustain me." Some even mentioned how husbands have come and gone, but their bonds of friendship with their women friends have remained intact. Despite hectic schedules, they have made time and saved energy to invest in friendship; in old age, they continue to build on these relationships, and they are well served by them. Friendships sometimes cross sex lines, as was made clear by one seventy-five-year-old divorced woman who spoke of "the joy of friendships" as what she liked most about being an older woman. She went on to say that, as she had grown older, she had found that both her male and female friendships had improved because "we can be more open and honest with each other."

Independence as another tool of survival involves several dimensions. Many women alluded to the notion that women, especially married women, should maintain some level of independence and separation from their husbands. They spoke of this independence as a sort of symbolic maintenance of separate identities. Two aspects were most frequently mentioned, namely, the economic and the social. Economic independence from husbands, as mentioned earlier, was born out of necessity; its importance had been taught to them as very young women through such parental admonitions as "Always have something of your own" and "Don't give every penny of your income to the family pot." The importance of economic independence was keenly demonstrated in the women's stories of divorce and separation. Financial independence had allowed safe exits from troubled marriages. However, other comments made clear that the need for separate identities had a social component as well. One retiree's comment illustrated this aspect and suggested a theme common to others when she said, "My husband and I don't feel that we have to depend on each other for social things, although we do things together. We are self-sufficient, we have balance." Thus, we see that social independence does not mean social isolation from one's spouse. It means maintaining dual social lives, that is, having one apart from the husband's, as well as one that is a part of the husband's. It means maintaining "balance."

Another dimension that undergirded their independence is more psychological in nature. This dimension is especially important because it provided the strength to persist when times got tough. First, the women learned to survive, to resist prejudice, and to develop an armor of resistance to negative messages. They learned to think of themselves as capable and smart women who were as good as anybody else. They learned to pick their battles because they could not win them all. They learned to take pride in their race, and they nurtured positive regard for being Black in defiance of society's message that they were inferior.

Lessons from the Present

When we look at the projected population statistics of the second and third decades of the twenty-first century, we see the extent to which baby boomers will swell the ranks of the aged in this society. Most of them will be women, and they will have spent decades in full-time employment. Most will reach retirement having established some level of economic independence, as well as having developed identities that encompass employment and motherhood. They will have lived lives often shaped by the stresses of juggling career and home, work and child rearing. In their later years, it is likely that they will shoulder major responsibility for the care of aging parents and relatives. Furthermore, they will grow old in a society that does not look favorably on the elderly, especially old women. In other words, they will face the challenges already faced by the women in our study

By most measures, the women we interviewed are living proof that it is possible for women who attain relative privilege—in terms of their prior location in the labor market—to retire from the world of paid labor with resources adequate to ensure a satisfactory quality of life. Their quality of life is also intimately connected to their good health and to the fact that they are active in retirement.

We believe that the aging process has been largely positive for these women "because of," rather than "in spite of," their race and gender. Their professional pursuits were shaped by their being African American and female. Almost all were involved in education or in serving the needs of others. The race uplift work that was embedded in the Black communities of segregation became second nature to them. Thus, much of their paid labor of the past is connected to their retirement pursuits of today. The unpaid work through which they make major contributions to young and old provides them a major outlet for their talents and interests. It also allows them to feel positive about their activities. For instance, among her many volunteer activities, a seventy-five-year-old retired college administrator talked about how she regularly drives three women in their eighties to their various errands every week. She also cooks Sunday dinner each week for one of them. As we discussed her high level of life satisfaction in retirement, she commented, "I am able to see some of the fruits of my labor by making others happy." As women who are very concerned about the future of the African

American community, their time is largely consumed by activities that are designed to express that interest.

There are two final elements to these women's lives in retirement that deserve mention. First, a lifetime of living and of meeting multiple challenges has given them the wisdom, "the wealth of experiences," as one described it, that accompanies aging. This wisdom was a central theme in our discussions of being old, and specifically of being old women. "I have sound advice and experiences that can be shared," was the way one retiree described her wisdom. Another woman used words that made clear that she had legacies to share with young people: "I have a lot of experiences to look back on and a lot to offer to young people." And then some women thought specifically in terms of what their earned wisdom meant for young African American women: "[I like] the experiences that I've had that I can share with younger women in order to help them cope because the hassles of life are behind me."

Finally, their life stories would be incomplete if we did not acknowledge the joie de vivre that characterizes their approach to living. Enjoying life was a recurrent theme in their discussions of aging and retirement. They engage in numerous activities that allow them to have fun, to feel vital, and to remain engaged. As testimony to the positive side of aging, a sixty-six-year-old woman, asked what she liked most about being an older woman, expressed a sentiment shared by many: "It's fun, and there aren't a lot of pressures or stresses in your life." Having things to look forward to is also important to these women's sense of vibrancy and well-being. Sometimes it is a trip planned with family or friends; sometimes it is a game of cards with friends that may go on well into the night; sometimes it is the goal of learning something new, as in the case of one seventy-two-year-old who planned to take a writing course. The positive anticipation of future events is not an aspect of the commonly held notion of the old in our society. Even though these women are well aware of their growing physical limitations, they look forward to the next five to ten years. An eighty-four-year-old spoke of how she hoped that in the next five to ten years "I will be as happy and contented as I am now." Another woman in her eighties expressed a similar sentiment about the future: "I hope that [my husband] and I have good mental and physical health and the sense of joy and well-being that we have now. [That we have] enough resources to share with someone else—a cause that can profit from us."

Being independent, positive, and forward looking, active in service to others—all are key elements in making the aging process a positive one for the women in this study. As African American women, they have lived long, rich lives that are testimony to their indominable spirit and to their "can do" attitude toward life as a double minority in American society. They live life to the fullest, and their regrets are few and far between. "Life has been good," as many of them testified.

Members of the dominant society often perceive that African Americans are never satisfied with this society, even when they attain some measure of success within it. Certainly, for these women such a perception is erroneous and belies the complexity of feelings that they, as recipients of discrimination, have toward their country. This point is illustrated powerfully in a conversation with a woman about her parents' attitudes toward America. Her comments provide a fitting end to our account of the lives of these African American pioneers. Recalling her parents' feelings for the United States, she said:

> [My parents] loved this country. Even though we suffered greatly from discrimination and segregation, they still loved America very, very much. And they taught us to love America. Of course, the thing that Black people in general—at that time and still—always wanted was [that] America be what it was supposed to be. You know, to live up to what was written in the Constitution and the Declaration of Independence.

Appendix
Researchers' Comments on the Study

Background

A number of years ago, we decided to combine our interests in women and gender (Slevin) and in gerontology (Wingrove) to devise a common ground. A focus on older women seemed a natural meeting point that recognized our collaborative interests. Fairly quickly, we became interested in a specific area of older women's lives, namely, retirement. We began to concentrate on topics surrounding the retirement of professional women. An extensive review and critique of the literature on women's retirement revealed several issues that troubled us.[1] Among them was the scarcity of studies on African American and professional women.

A qualitative study of retired African American women who had lifelong professional careers suggested itself for a number of reasons. Aside from there being few such investigations, we liked the idea of committing our time and energies to exploring the lives of a group of women whom we perceived as both pioneers and role models for today's professional women. Also, conversations with personal friends and professional colleagues who were African American women convinced us that this study was one we should conduct. All felt that our inquiry would make an important contribution to the legacy of their race, and to women of all races, by listening to the voices of women who had been pioneers in professional fields at a time when racial and gender barriers were pervasive. The need to capture the experiences of a special group of women before it was too late was a compelling argument for proceeding quickly. These women also argued that a combination of their sponsorship plus our open interpersonal styles would ensure an adequate sample of women and create the right atmosphere so that participants would speak openly to us about their lives. In the end, the fact that so many African American women encouraged us and were willing to help us with their advice and time added to our resolve and commitment to complete this study. We have done our best to honor their confidence in us.

Concerns of Race and Gender

A major concern for us was the fact that we were White scholars trying to understand the experiences of minority women. Both of us were committed to being constructively sensitive to our majority status. We knew that we would have to be especially careful to design the study in ways that both recognized potential problems and included built-in safeguards that would help minimize the likelihood of producing distorted information. To this end, we solicited the help and advice of an African American colleague with a Ph.D. in the social sciences who consulted with us on research design, interview construction, and, later, the interpretation of our analyses. We remain in her debt.

We were especially sensitive to the extent to which African American informants might think of our academic research as being exploitative.[2] Because our participants were so highly educated, and because so many of them had earned advanced degrees in the social sciences, we knew they would be especially tuned in to this possibility. We had lengthy conversations with a number of them about the study, its methodology, and our motivation for conducting it. We believe that had they sensed insincerity or exploitation on our part, they would have called a halt to the interviews. Additional evidence of their comfort level with the researchers and with the study itself is the fact that almost all returned lengthy questionnaires that they completed after the interviews.

As our biographical profiles show, one of us who was born and grew to adulthood in Ireland (Slevin) could use what Margaret Andersen refers to as the tension of personal cultural identity to help "examine critically majority experiences and beliefs."[3] Slevin's foreign status often highlighted differences that led the informants to spend time explaining, among other things, race relations in the United States.

We came to realize after a few interviews that the gender of the interviewer made a difference in some cases. A number of women voluntarily discussed selected aspects of their sexual lives with the male interviewer in response to, for example, questions about the advantages and disadvantages of being an older woman.[4] None discussed this issue with the female interviewer. However, the women were more likely to discuss "second shift" issues when they were talking to the female interviewer. Finally, because we were committed to addressing what Shulamit Reinharz calls, "the difficulties . . . of writing about a living person in a way that satisfies both parties," we asked several of the women who participated in the study to read final drafts of the book and to give us their view of how well we captured and interpreted their lives.[5] Ensuing discussions led to revisions of our thinking in particular instances that are reflected in the final analysis.

Interviews

The available literature provided guidance as we decided what broad questions to ask. However, we were careful not to devise interview schedules that were overly structured. As Norman Denzin reminds us, one of the positive aspects of using more open-ended life history interviews is that they allow for human conduct to "be studied and understood from the perspective of the persons involved."[6] Here again, our African American colleague and consultant proved invaluable as she often made suggestions about questions to be included and how they should be worded.

As already mentioned in the Introduction, we conducted topical life histories. We concentrated on gaining broad pictures of three phases of these African American professional women's lives, namely, their early family and educational lives, their employment, and their retirements. We asked about their pasts as recalled in memories of family, community, church, and school. Their occupational histories and the challenges and opportunities they had faced as African American women in their chosen careers were discussed, as were their present lives in retirement from paid employment. We talked to them about growing old, and we asked them to reflect on the advantages and disadvantages of being older women in a society that denigrates old age. We also spoke to them about their sense of the future, particularly as African American women with expressed concerns for the Black American community at large.

Throughout our discussions, we were conscious of seeking the threads of connection among the various phases of their lives. We also tried to probe and to have the women reflect on the connections among race, class, gender, and age in their lives. We were aware of the need to pay attention to the silences as well as to the spoken words. We encouraged each woman to tell her story in her own way. We did not try to force chronology during the telling of a story, although sometimes we did have to go back and ask about the ordering of events. Heeding the advice of feminist researchers, we tried to encourage the women to take liberties and to digress within the limits of the broad topics that guided our interviews.[7] Conversations were filled with anecdotes, which they seemed to delight in telling and which we thoroughly enjoyed hearing.

Creating a Collective Biography

Our interviews produced more than twelve hundred pages of transcripts.[8] The women also completed a questionnaire that sought information on a variety of topics, including background demographic information, their current activities, and their attitudes toward a variety of issues. Together, the interviews and the questionnaire provide the raw material that allowed us to create a collective biography of these fifty women. Collective biographies, by their nature, present inevitable tensions for both researchers and readers. In our case, we use narratives from individual life stories in order to illustrate collective themes, creating a certain unavoidable but creative tension between the personal and the anonymous.[9]

In making sense of data that have a central focus that is autobiographical in nature, the issue of how a person recalls past events, particularly when those events are inevitably seen through the lens of the present, raises concerns for researchers. These concerns may be especially strong when the topics under investigation are controversial or command strong emotion. When people are asked to reconstruct the past through the eyes and ears of current knowledge and awareness, reinterpretation is inevitable, especially in a sample of well-educated women who are being asked to discuss issues such as legal segregation and race and gender discrimination.

Asking someone to remember her earlier life invites her inescapably to use the lens of lived experience to reconstruct the past. For example, when discussing racial inequality and race relations in their early childhoods, the retirees frequently followed a description of the discrimination faced by African Americans in those days with the words "That's the way things were; we didn't know any different *then*" (authors' emphasis added). Similarly, as they looked back on the discrimination that they faced because they were women, a number of them commented on the fact that awareness of gender inequities was not part of their consciousness earlier in their lives. "We were not into the gender thing then" were the words one woman used to explain that many aspects of gender inequality were invisible to them during their youth. The issue of reinterpretation also affects the social construction of class. The recall of one's earlier life, particularly if it was lived in poverty, is invariably affected when one reconstructs that life from a current vantage point of relative affluence. Hence, as many of these women recalled their childhoods, they frequently commented, "We were poor then, but we didn't know it."

Since reconstruction of the past seems inevitable, the question of accuracy arises, especially when we called on respondents to remember past events in their lives, which spanned at least six decades. However, because our central focus was the lives of a particular group of women as seen from their perspective, and because we were committed to allowing their voices to interpret their lives, we assumed that the women we interviewed told their stories as they saw fit. In fact, it is precisely their interpretations of their life experiences that form the essence of this study. Our task was to analyze and to give voice to their subjective experiences. In this regard, the insight of the feminist historian Mary Jo Maynes is worth quoting at some length:

> In the final analysis, however, the line between lived experience and memory of experience, while impossible to draw, is for many purposes not relevant. Since people act not on the basis of unassimilated facts of an existence but on the basis of the sense they make of a particular experience within the context of a lifetime, for many analytical purposes recorded memories are the pertinent evidence. Moreover, the whole-life perspective and the interplay between past and present that characterize life stories are precisely what makes them so valuable. They are, simply put, causal arguments about the forces that made a particular life turn out the way it did.[10]

Another feminist historian, Luisa Passerini, argues that "all autobiographical memory is true. It is up to the interpreter to discover in which sense, where, and for which purpose."[11]

The Issue of Social Class

We provide a picture of the early economic circumstances of these women by using the family that they lived with for most of their early lives as the foundation for judgment. In the majority of cases we are referring to biological parents. We cannot say definitively, however, how many sources of income went into a particular family's income "pot." Some families had help from extended family members; others had children (grown as well as the young) who contributed to the family income; and still others took in boarders who helped them make ends meet.

According to their self-descriptions, twenty-one of these women grew up poor. While the vast majority of them did not go hungry, they did live fairly close to the edge. Most often their fathers were laborers and their mothers domestics or laundresses. This pattern of mothers' employment and its importance to family survival is one that distinguishes African American families from the majority of White families during this particular time. By contrast, twenty-three of the women in the study were from families whose economic circumstances were typically described as "comfortable." In these instances, there were few luxuries, but there was also no daily struggle to acquire basic necessities. Fathers worked in skilled or semiskilled jobs or were self-employed as farmers or small-store owners. A few were teachers. In this middle group, mothers' occupations ranged from domestic or other service work to teacher, but nine of the twenty-three mothers were primarily homemakers. Mothers' paid employment in the "comfortable" group, while important, was not essential, as it was in the case of poor families. Finally, four women characterized their family of orientation as affluent. For these few women, luxuries were a reality, and they lived a lifestyle that included paid help in the home, travel, and access to expensive entertainment. Three fathers owned considerable property and business, while one was a physician. Mothers were homemakers or teachers. In two remaining cases, the women described their families as socially mobile during their childhoods.

One's family moved from relative poverty to affluence. For the other, it was the reverse; the mother, who had been a teacher before marriage, was forced to become a laundry worker upon her husband's death.

In many ways, this description of family economic backgrounds is deceptively simple. By design, we do not use standard socioeconomic indicators, which are overwhelmingly based on White male experiences.[12] To do so would falsely imply comparable labor force experiences. As the sociologist Andrew Billingsley reminds us, "The shadows of the plantation which linger in both the opportunity structure of the wider society and the capabilities of the Negro people are most glaringly reflected in family income."[13] Because of the racist economy, it was not unusual for fathers to work jobs that for White men would have been considered inappropriate for their educational level. For example, at least one father who was a college graduate worked as a postal worker. Another father moved from teaching to selling insurance to loading ships. Finally, it was not unusual for fathers to work two or more jobs at disparate positions on the occupational ladder.

An Overarching Theme

As we listened to the women of our study talk, the notion of survival and resistance emerged as an overarching theme in their life stories. Whether they were talking about lessons they had learned in the home, church, and school or describing the strategies they used in their everyday work lives, we discovered that the major guiding principle of their lives could be subsumed under the broad theme of *survival and resistance*.[14] Their achievements and their successful careers are testaments to their ability to resist and to survive in inhospitable climates. Even though adaptation was a key to their survival and success, it would be wrong to think of these women as passive recipients of oppression. Each is a survivor who responded to forces of oppression in a variety of ways. Sometimes survival requires acceptance of things that cannot be changed; at other times resistance itself defines survival. Cumulative experiences with discrimination helped them negotiate both structural and personal constraints. Thus, a lifetime of experience with oppression provided them with road maps to guide their paths. Taught in early childhood to "pick their battles," they navigated oppression without accepting it and without being consumed by it. In this sense, their lives are graphic testimonies to perseverance, strength, and adaptability.

The Authors

There is no question that our own biographies influenced the project. Some factors deserve brief note. Kate Slevin grew up as a member of the Catholic minority in Northern Ireland prior to the civil rights movement in that country. Her father was involved for several decades in the political fight for minority rights. While somewhat protected from the harshness of a blatantly discriminatory system by virtue of her middle-class family background, she had, nevertheless, a number of experiences that made it easy for her to personally identify with the African American women in this study. For example, she attended totally segregated schools. Despite residence in the United States that now exceed twenty years, she still feels that her perspective as a member of the White majority is one akin to what feminists call the "outsider-within."[15] In addition, she also brought to the project a career-long commitment to feminism and the feminist perspective. Finally, as a professional woman who is also a wife and mother of two children, she was keenly attuned to "second shift" issues as they arose in the interviews and the subsequent data analysis.

C. Ray Wingrove has devoted much of his career to the field of social gerontology. He has conducted a number of studies involving older women and has paid particular attention to the development of techniques effective in interviewing the elderly. He grew up in the rural South and witnessed Black American women working in the homes and fields of Whites. He remembers visiting Black tenant farmers as a child with his grandfather, who often approached White employers in an advocacy role for the tenant families. His memories of their social and economic circumstances coincide with many of the stories told by the women depicted in this book.

Notes

NOTES TO THE INTRODUCTION

1. Most of the women in this study referred to themselves as Black. Throughout this book we use "African American," "Black American," and "Black" interchangeably.

2. Diane Gibson, "Broken Down by Age and Gender: 'The Problem of Old Women' Redefined," *Gender and Society* 10 (August 1996), and Jacquelyne Johnson Jackson, "Aging Black Women and Public Policies," *Black Scholar* 19 (May/June 1988).

3. Jacquelyne Johnson Jackson, "Aging Black Women," 31.

4. Irma McClaurin-Allen, "Incongruities: Dissonance and Contradiction in the Life of a Black Middle-Class Woman," in Faye Ginsburg and Anna Lowenhaupt Tsing (eds.), *Uncertain Terms: Negotiating Gender in American Culture* (Boston: Beacon Press, 1990), 330.

5. Eleanor Palo Stoller and Rose Campbell Gibson, *Worlds of Difference: Inequality in the Aging Experience* (Thousand Oaks, Calif.: Pine Forge Press, 1994), xxvii.

6. Ibid., 7–8.

NOTES TO CHAPTER I

1. For further discussion of the continued salience of race over class, see Lois Benjamin's *The Black Elite: Facing the Color Line in the Twilight of the Twentieth Century* (Chicago: Nelson-Hall, 1991).

2. Paradoxical as it may seem today, gender inequality went largely unchallenged by women of all races at this time. For the women we studied, questioning racism as an unjust system was reinforced by family and community. By contrast, gender inequality was not seen as unjust. It was *taught* within the family.

3. For a powerful description of the role Jim Crow laws played in the

lives of Southern Blacks, see Mamie Garvin Field and Karen Field's *Lemon Swamp and Other Places* (New York: Free Press, 1983). They describe how Jim Crow played "like a background Muzak unlistened to," while Blacks managed to maintain an emotional detachment to racist encounters.

4. Irma McClaurin-Allen, "Incongruities: Dissonance and Contradiction in the Life of a Black Middle-Class Woman," in Faye Ginsburg and Anna Lowenhaupt Tsing (eds.), *Uncertain Terms: Negotiating Gender in American Culture* (Boston: Beacon Press, 1990), 315–333.

5. This attitude is aptly captured in the words of Gloria Wade-Gayles in *Pushed Back to Strength: A Black Woman's Journey Home* (Boston: Beacon Press, 1993), 90. She recalls her own childhood growing up in the segregated South: "If we had to be virtuous and modest because we were black, we had to be all the more so because we lived in a housing project. Race, gender and class were the axes on which our socialization turned. There was always something we had to prove because of where we lived. . . . Just because people thought we couldn't achieve and couldn't be virtuous meant, in the minds of our parents, that we had to be. We had to be the exception to all assumptions, all rumors, all myths, all predictions about failure."

6. Gerda Lerner, ed., *Black Women in White America: A Documentary History* (New York: Pantheon Books, 1972), xxiv.

7. A racist and sexist economy ensured that Black women could more readily find work at the lowest rungs of the economic ladder than could Black men, and, therefore, they were often forced to be self-supporting. This contrasts with the lives of most White women at that time. For African American women, whatever their social class, there was an acute awareness that a racist economy meant that each person must be self-reliant. Women must be able to survive alone or, if married, contribute to the family's survival. Such independence was accompanied by certain paradoxes. On the one hand, Black women had to work, married or single, because of economic necessity. On the other hand, the inevitable independence and self-reliance that resulted was often used by White society against them; they were falsely denigrated as "matriarchs."

NOTES TO CHAPTER 2

1. See, for example, E. Franklin Frazier, *The Negro in the United States,* rev. (New York: Macmillan, 1957).

2. Andrew Billingsley makes this point in *Black Families in White America* (Englewood Cliffs, N.J.: Prentice-Hall, 1986), 126.

3. All the women emphasized how, during this era of segregation, Black teachers felt a special responsibility for the children they taught and mentored. This is discussed in detail in chapter 3.

4. Earlier social scientists, both Black and White, often erroneously described a female-dominated or matriarchal system in Black communities.

5. For a particularly interesting discussion of Black women's invisibility as leaders a few decades later, see Bernice McNair Barnett, "Invisible Southern Black Women Leaders in the Civil Rights Movement: The Triple Constraints of Gender, Race and Class," *Gender and Society* 7 (June 1993), 162–182.

6. The sociologist Erving Goffman first used the concepts of frontstage and backstage in *The Presentation of Self in Everyday Life* (Garden City, N.Y.: Doubleday, 1959). We borrow Goffman's terms but use them differently. Our emphasis is not on individual presentations of self in social interactions but rather on structured inequality. We use the terms to convey that women are relegated to backstage or behind-the-scenes activities, while men are allowed to be front stage in the public eye.

7. In both White and Black communities, women were permitted "frontstage" roles when men's energies were directed elsewhere. For example, one woman recalled how, during World War II, her mother was the leader of a bond drive in her community.

8. In their book *Black Metropolis* (New York: Harper and Row, 1962), St. Clair Drake and Horace Cayton used the term "race man" to describe those men in segregated communities who felt responsible for representing Blacks to the dominant White society in a positive light.

9. Such tightly integrated communities were characterized by relationships based on kinship, family, and personal ties. The German sociologist Ferdinand Toennies described this phenomenon as "gemeinschaft." What is uniquely racialized in the context of these Black American communities, however, is their response to the structural constraints of legal segregation.

10. See Elijah Anderson's discussion of female "old heads" in *Street Wise* (Chicago: University of Chicago Press, 1990), 73.

11. In discussions of our study, several African American colleagues asked if most of the women interviewed were "light skinned." We neither systematically noted nor recorded the skin color of the women interviewed.

12. For a discussion of the complexities of both Black and White

attitudes toward color in this era, see Lawrence W. Levine, *Black Culture and Black Consciousness* (Oxford: Oxford University Press, 1978), 284.

13. Other scholars have noted similar tensions for Black parents, historically as well as currently. John Scanzoni's book *The Black Family in Modern America* (Boston: Allyn and Bacon, 1971) supports these observations.

NOTES TO CHAPTER 3

1. Franklin E. Frazier, *The Negro Church in America* (New York: Schocken Books, 1963), 8.

2. For an in-depth discussion of the dual role that religion has historically played for African Americans, see, for example, Gary T. Marx, *Protest and Prejudice: A Study of Belief in the Black Community* (New York: Harper and Row, 1967).

3. Martin Luther King, *Stride Toward Freedom* (New York: Ballantine Books, 1958), 28–29.

4. In addition to Frazier's *The Negro Church in America*, see also Benjamin Mays and Joseph W. Nicholson, *The Negro's Church* (New York: Institute of Social and Religious Research, 1933); H. M. Nelson and A. K. Nelson, *Black Church in the Sixties* (Lexington: University of Kentucky Press, 1975); Dionne J. Jones and William H. Matthews (eds.), *The Black Church: A Community Resource* (Washington, D.C.: Institute for Urban Affairs and Research, Howard University, 1977); and A. J. Raboteau, *Slave Religion: The "Invisible Institution" in the Antebellum South* (New York: Oxford University Press, 1978).

5. Katie Geneva Cannon, "The Emergence of Black Feminist Consciousness," Letty M. Russell (ed.), in *Feminist Interpretations of the Bible* (Philadelphia: Westminster Press, 1985), 34.

6. Gloria Wade-Gayles, *Pushed Back to Strength: A Black Woman's Journey Home* (Boston: Beacon Press, 1993), 104–105.

7. As Cannon in "The Emergence of Black Feminist Consciousness," p. 30, says, "The Black church is the crucible through which the systematic faith affirmations and the principles of biblical interpretation have been revealed."

8. See Frazier, *The Negro Church*.

9. Speaking of her parents' generation and the racialized discipline that was required for survival, Kristin Hunter Lattany writes, "They were proud

of being black and of associating with black achievers; wary and watchful of whites, yet strictly disciplined so as to be acceptable to them, and scathing in their scorn for blacks who were not so minded and so disciplined." "Off-Timing to the Different Drummer," in Gerald Early (ed.), *Lure and Loathing: Essays on Race, Identity, and the Ambivalence of Assimilation* (New York: Penguin Books, 1993), 165.

10. Bernice McNair Barnett, "Invisible Southern Black Women Leaders in the Civil Rights Movement: The Triple Constraints of Gender, Race and Class," *Gender and Society* 7 (June 1993): 175.

11. For a more thorough discussion of how doing gender means doing deference, see Jennifer L. Pierce, *Gender Trials: Emotional Lives in Contemporary Law Firms* (Berkeley: University of California Press, 1995), and Arlene Kaplan Daniels's review in *Contemporary Sociology* 26 (March 1997): 136–138.

NOTES TO CHAPTER 4

1. See, for example, Paula Giddings, *When and Where I Enter* (New York: Bantam Books, 1984).

2. For a more in-depth discussion of the economic constraints faced by Black Americans in this era, see John Sibley Butler, "Myrdal Revisited: The Negro in Business," *Daedalus* 124:1 (Winter 1995): 199–221.

3. Black teachers, as representatives of the middle class, were important bridges between the Black community and the larger White society. They were the links to upward mobility.

4. See Patricia A. Edwards, "Before and After School Desegregation: African-American Parents' Involvement in Schools," *Educational Policy* 7:3 (September 1993): 354.

5. The philosophy of this approach to teaching was particularly centered in the Black experience. It was one that many of these women later continued in their own lives as teachers. We also see elements of it in their retirement activities. In this sense, they completed in their adult lives a circle that had begun in their childhoods.

6. Paula Giddings writes, "Morals and education were also deemed necessary if Blacks were to emerge from the pit of poverty. Rising out of poverty would in turn benefit the entire race." Giddings, *When and Where I Enter*, 101.

1. The sociologist Elizabeth Higginbotham describes Black American professional women as "colonized professionals" because they have disproportionately offered their professional services within the confines of the African American community. They also have been concentrated in the female-dominated professions of teaching, nursing, and social work. See Elizabeth Higginbotham, *Work and Survival for Black Women Research Paper 1* (Memphis: Center for Research on Women, Memphis State University, 1984).

2. See Judith M. Gerson and Kathy Peiss, "Boundaries, Negotiation, Consciousness: Reconceptualizing Gender Relations," *Social Problems* 32:4 (April 1985): 317–331. Using Gerson and Peiss's continuum, these women were at one end of the gender consciousness continuum. Certainly, they were aware of gender—in other words, they could provide "a non-critical description of the existing system of gender relations" (324). However, they had not arrived at a level of gender consciousness that Gerson and Peiss describe as feminist/antifeminist consciousness. This point represents the other end of the consciousness continuum and involves an articulated ideology of challenge or defense of the existing system of gender relations.

3. In response to a question about how things might have been different for her had she been a man, another woman, who also had dreamed about being a lawyer, provided an interesting comparison between her own generation of professional African American women and her daughter's. She said, "My daughter's a lawyer. Yeah, as a matter of fact, we [have] six in her generation in the family that are lawyers."

4. For the most part, they could provide their expertise only to the members of their own economically strapped communities.

5. Even if married, Black American women knew that a discriminatory system would rarely provide Black men with the income necessary to be the sole financial support of a family. Paula Giddings points out that during the Second World War and after, White families needed the additional incomes of wives, but Black families found them even more essential. See Paula Giddings, *When and Where I Enter* (New York: Bantam Books, 1984), 232.

6. See, for example, James D. Anderson, *The Education of Blacks in the South, 1860–1935* (Chapel Hill: University of North Carolina Press, 1988), and also Robert A. Margo, *Race and Schooling in the South* (Chicago: University of Chicago Press, 1990).

7. Vanessa Siddle Walker's recent study of an African American school

community in the South during segregation also reinforces our attention to these positive outcomes. In particular, she cites the positive learning environment provided by Black teachers and principals. See Vanessa Siddle Walker, *Their Highest Potential: An African American School Community in the Segregated South* (Chapel Hill: University of North Carolina Press, 1996).

8. Patricia Hill Collins, *Black Feminist Thought* (Boston: Unwin Hyman, 1990), 147.

9. Cheryl Townsend Gilkes, among others, has explored the special role Black American women have historically played in this regard. See Cheryl Townsend Gilkes, "Together and in Harness: Women's Traditions in the Sanctified Church," *Signs*, 10:4 (Summer 1985): 678–699.

10. In discussing the history of women's special commitment to education in the Black community, Patricia Hill Collins notes, "Like their anonymous slave foremothers, these women saw the activist potential of education and skillfully used this Black female sphere of influence to foster a definition of education as a cornerstone of Black community development." Collins, *Black Feminist Thought*, 147.

11. For further discussion of the subordination of Black women in the African American community see ibid., 86.

12. The salaries at Black universities have historically been much lower than those at comparable White universities, a fact that further compounds the salary discrimination experienced by Black women.

13. This had two additional long-term negative consequences. It affected the point of entry on the salary scale for her next job, and it set a pattern of reduced salary that ultimately influenced her pension. This pattern, of course, was true for all the women in this study.

14. For an in-depth analysis of how middle-class Black life continues to be haunted by racism, see Joe R. Feagin, "The Continuing Significance of Race: Antiblack Discrimination in Public Places," *American Sociological Review* 56 (February 1991): 101–116.

NOTES TO CHAPTER 6

1. For a discussion of this kind of work experience, see Suzanne C. Carothers, "Catching Sense: Learning from Our Mothers to be Black and Female," in Faye Ginsburg and Anna Lowenhaupt Tsing (eds.), *Uncertain Terms: Negotiating Gender in American Culture* (Boston: Beacon Press, 1990), 242.

2. See *A Portrait of Older Minorities* (Washington, D.C.: American Association of Retired Persons, 1992), 2–3.

3. Elizabeth M. Heidbreder, "Factors in Retirement Adjustment: White-Collar/Blue-Collar Experience," *Industrial Gerontology* 12 (1972): 69–79.

4. Although these incomes may seem modest, with one exception all of the women in this study, both single and married, had household incomes that put them well above the median U.S. household income in 1993. See Judith Treas, "Older Americans in the 1990s and Beyond," *Population Bulletin* 50:2 (May 1995): 27.

5. C. Ray Wingrove and Kathleen F. Slevin, "A Sample of Professional and Managerial Women's Success in Work and Retirement," *Journal of Women and Aging* 3:2 (1991): 95–117.

6. For further discussion of this pattern of socialization, see Carothers, "Catching Sense," 243.

7. We are grateful to Toni Calasanti, who first suggested this type of analysis to us.

8. Rose C. Gibson, "Blacks in an Aging Society," *Daedalus* 115 (Winter 1986): 349–371.

9. Robert C. Atchley, *Social Forces and Aging,* 7th ed. (Belmont, Calif.: Wadsworth, 1994), 326–327.

10. Ibid., 362.

11. See Paula Giddings, *In Search of Sisterhood: Delta Sigma Theta and the Challenge of the Black Sorority Movement* (New York: Morrow, 1988).

12. William C. Cockerham, *This Aging Society*, 2nd ed. (Upper Saddle River, N.J.: Prentice-Hall, 1997), 134–135.

13. Ibid., 138.

14. For a discussion of contemporary anti-Black discrimination, see Joe R. Feagin, "The Continuing Significance of Race: Antiblack Discrimination in Public Places," *American Sociological Review* 56 (February 1991): 101–116.

NOTES TO THE APPENDIX

1. See Kathleen F. Slevin and C. Ray Wingrove, "Women in Retirement: A Review and Critique of Empirical Research since 1976," *Sociological Inquiry* 65 (February 1995): 1–20.

2. See Margaret L. Andersen, "Studying Across Difference: Race, Class,

and Gender in Qualitative Research," in John H. Stanfield and Rutledge M. Dennis (eds.), *Race and Ethnicity in Research Methods* (Newbury Park, Calif.: Sage, 1993), 48.

3. Ibid.

4. There is also the possibility that the age difference between the female interviewer and the retired women was a factor here. These sorts of issues, while sociologically important and intriguing, are not the main focus of this book. For this reason, we mention them but do not dwell extensively on them.

5. The feminist Margaret Andersen discusses this issue in Shulamit Reinharz, *Feminist Methods in Social Research* (New York: Oxford University Press, 1992), 132.

6. Norman K. Denzin, *The Research Act: A Theoretical Introduction to Sociological Methods* (New York: McGraw-Hill, 1978), 216.

7. See, for example, Katheryn Anderson et al., "Beginning Where We Are: Feminist Methodology in Oral History," in Joyce McCarl Nielsen (ed.), *Feminist Research Methods: Exemplary Readings in the Social Sciences* (Boulder, Colo.: Westview Press, 1990), 94–112.

8. All transcribing was done by an African American woman.

9. We grappled with the issue of giving each woman a pseudonym, but it became so cumbersome that we abandoned it. In all cases where the names of people or places are used, they are fictionalized in order to protect identities. Furthermore, in the telling of a woman's story, we occasionally altered details in a way that did not change the point of her story but ensured that she could not be identified.

10. Mary Jo Maynes, "Autobiography and Class Formation in Nineteenth-Century Europe: Methodological Considerations," *Social Science History* 16:3 (Fall 1992): 522.

11. Linda Passerini, "Women's Personal Narratives: Myths, Experiences and Emotions," in Personal Narratives Group (eds.), *Interpreting Women's Lives* (Bloomington: Indiana University Press, 1989), 189–197.

12. Andrew Billingsley points to the problems that result from using White indices of social class to understand the situation of Blacks. This is particularly problematic, he argues, at the lower social status levels, where the very utility of describing Black families in standard social-class terms is questionable. He cautions that, while some indicators may provide a description of patterns of association, they are still "completely inadequate and inappropriate for describing behavior or values or preferences or styles

of life or child rearing patterns in the Negro community." Andrew Billingsley, *Black Families in White America* (Englewood Cliffs, N.J.: Prentice-Hall, 1986), 124.

13. Ibid.

14. For an extensive analysis of the unique aspects of Black women's survival and resistance, see Kesho Yvonne Scott, *The Habit of Surviving: Black Women's Strategies for Life* (New Brunswick, N.J.: Rutgers University Press, 1991).

15. See Patricia Hill Collins, "Learning from the Outsider Within: The Sociological Significance of Black Feminist Thought," *Social Problems* 33:6 (1968): 14–32.

Index

affirmative action, 88, 114
African American women: image, 6; myths, 6
African-Methodist church, 53. *See also* church
age of participants. *See* study participants
aging, attitudes toward, 147, 148
"American Dream," 16; racism, influences of, 17; segregation, influences of, 17
Anderson, Margaret, 163
apartheid, 22–23
avoidance of White Americans, 14–16

baby boomers, 5–6
"backstage" negotiations, 36, 37
Baptist church, 49, 53. *See also* church
bias. *See* gender discrimination; racial discrimination
Billingsley, Andrew, 168
birth order, effect on education level, 71–72
Black American women. *See* African American women
Black history, 76
Black schools: classroom autonomy, 92; class size, 92; community involvement, 80, 94; holistic approach to teaching, 96, 97; inequality, 80–81; inferiority of, 4, 91; stereotypes of Black intelligence, 93–94; teachers, respect for, 92; teachers' roles, 80, 81, 82, 83, 91–92; "uplift work," 93; White policy, 93; White school boards, 79
Black women. *See* African American women

Cannon, Katie Geneva, 50
career: choice limitations, 88–89; gender limitations, 85, 86, 89 (*see also* gender discrimination); nursing, 91; occupational hierarchy, 114, 115; professionals, Black, 35, 36, 38; race limitations, 84, 89 (*see also* racial discrimination); "race work," 93; salary inequity, 90–91; social work, 91, 96; "uplift work," 93. *See also* study participants; work
chaperons, 19
child-rearing, as community effort, 41–44. *See also* parenting
church, 8; African-Methodist, 53; attendance, expectations of, 53; Baptist, 49, 53; and community life, relationship between, 50–51, 52–54; as empowering institution, 55; and family, relationship between, 50, 51, 52; gender hierarchy, 61–62; gender-specific behavior, 59–61, 62, 64; gender tensions, 29, 61, 62, 100; importance of, 49; leadership roles for Black women, 36, 56, 58; Methodist, 49, 53; moral standards preached, 51; multiple affiliations, 53–54; pooled resources to build, 55; and Reconstruction, relationship between, 50;

church (continued)
  reinforcement of community norms,
    60–61; religious profiles of intervie-
    wees, 49; retirement, role during,
    138–140; sacredness of Sundays, 53;
    secular functions, 55–56; segrega-
    tion, role during, 55–56; as shaper,
    56–59; slavery, role during, 50; social
    change, as agent of, 50; social class
    tensions, 61, 62; social life, 54–55,
    64; tensions within, 61–64; "uplift"
    activities, 141; women in leadership
    roles, 1, 36
civil rights movement, 155. See also de-
    segregation
class, social: childhood experiences, ef-
    fect on, 15–16; protections offered
    by, 15; and race, intersection of, 27;
    skin color differences, 63; symmetry,
    74; system, 12–13; tensions, 61, 62;
    and work ethic, relationship be-
    tween, 26–27
cohort analysis, 7, 8, 88
Collins, Patricia Hill, 93
communal child-rearing. See commu-
    nity life; parenting
community life, 8; and children, impor-
    tance of, 41 (see also parenting);
    church as social center, 54–55, 64
    (see also church); church-reinforce-
    ment of norms, 60–61; ethos of shar-
    ing, 37–38, 38–41; food sharing,
    38–39; as foundation, 33, 48; gender,
    influence of, 36, 37; health care,
    40–41; quality of life, 37; sacrifice
    for a common good, 39; under segre-
    gation, 34 (see also segregation);
    skills sharing, 40; social life, 54–55,
    64; social problems, 44–45; status,
    35, 36; teachers, respect for, 35–36,
    92; tensions, 44–47; "uplift" activi-
    ties, 140, 141, 142, 157; volun-
    teerism by Black women, 33–34;
    women's contributions, 33–34, 36,
    39, 40–41, 42–43

conflict, avoiding with Whites, 21–22.
    See also resistance
confrontation, avoiding with Whites,
    21. See also resistance
cultural milieus, separate, 12–13

desegregation: discrimination post-
    1960s, 109–110; of facilities, 108;
    job loss following, 110; laws address-
    ing discrimination, 118, 119; loss of
    employment stature following, 111;
    teaching experiences, 108. See also
    racial discrimination
discipline, 43, 57
discrimination. See gender discrimina-
    tion; racial discrimination

economic independence, 155–156,
    157; Black girls vs. White girls, 28;
    necessity, 26, 30–31; for separate
    identity, 30
economics: and church, relationship be-
    tween, 55–56; cooperation among
    Blacks, 55; opportunities, limited,
    74; vulnerability of Blacks, 38. See
    also economic independence
education: birth-order and expecta-
    tions, 71–72; boarding schools, 68,
    70; economic motivation, 74–75;
    family support, 73; gender limita-
    tions, 84, 85, 86; importance in
    Black community, 35–36, 56, 65–66,
    67, 68; leaving home for, 68–69, 70;
    limited opportunities, 12; motiva-
    tors, 73–75; in the "North," 65, 70;
    public vs. parochial schools, 68, 81;
    racial limitations, 84–85; restric-
    tions, 65; sacrifices to attain, 71–72;
    segregation, effects of, 8; as survival
    tool, 154; teachers, respect for,
    35–36; teachers as motivators, 73;
    uprooting family for, 65, 70. See
    also Black schools; racial discrimina-
    tion
"emotional sanctuary" from racism, 16

family: influence during formative years, 11; setting, 8; support system, 71. *See also* education; parenting, emphasis on education

fathers, relationships with daughters, 19

feminist perspective, 8

"frontstage" negotiations, 36, 37

gender: approaches to teaching, 95–96; -based career choices, 85–86; hierarchy, within church, 61–62; as influence on transactions with Whites, 36–37; and race, relationship between, 11–12, 30; restrictions on boys vs. girls, 18–19; -specific codes of conduct, 59–61; stratification, 36; tensions, 29, 61, 62, 100. *See also* gender discrimination

gender discrimination: career, 89; career limitations, 84, 85, 86, 89; class action suit, 101–102; deference to male colleagues, 98; elementary and middle school academic settings, 100–101; female work environments, 97; high school academic settings, 101–102; pensions, effect on, 102; post-high school academic settings, 98, 99–100; post-1960s experiences, 115–188; promotions, 99–100; retirement income, effect on, 129; workload differences, 99

geographical identity of study participants. *See* study participants

Gibson, Rose, 7, 137

health care, in Black community, 40–41

hostility, 20–21

independence, 155

institutional racism, 12. *See also* racism; segregation

integration. *See* desegregation

integrity, 22, 24

intelligence: stereotypes regarding Black, 93, 94; value placed on, 76, 77, 78, 79

interviewees. *See* study participants

interviews: criteria of, 2; pilot, 2; sample size, 3. *See also* study participants

Jackson, Jacquelyne, 6

Jim Crow laws, 120

King, Martin Luther, Jr., 50, 106

legal segregation. *See* segregation

light-skinned Blacks, 45–46, 63

manual labor *vs.* professional career, 66, 67

marriage, 28–29; virginity, 19

Maynes, Mary Jo, 166

McClaurin-Allen, Irma, 7, 16

mentors, 22, 25; study participants as, 143, 144

Methodist church, 49, 53. *See also* church

moral standards, 51; sexual mores, 18–19

motherhood combined with work, 5–6. *See also* mothers

mothers: influence on daughters, 17; message of economic independence, 29; support for daughters' educations, 72–73, 83

mutual aid societies, 55–56

Native American ancestry, 45

networking, 155

nonresistance, 21–22. *See also* resistance

nonviolence, 23

oppression, 6–7; experiences of elders, 13

parenting: and African American survival, importance to, 11; American Dream, ideals of, 16–17; chaperons, 19; church-going, insistence on, 53;

parenting *(continued)*
creativity in teaching children, 12, 30; demands for excellence, 16–18; emphasis on education, 67–68; influence during formative years, 11; lessons on "being the best," 25–26; reinforcement of school lessons, 83; schools, involvement in, 80; scriptural basis, 51–52; sexual mores, 18–19; shielding children from racist encounters, 14, 15–16; shielding children from segregation, 14; strictness with daughters, 19–20, 47; surrogate, 69, 70, 94. *See also* family

part-time work, 26

Passerini, Luisa, 166

patriarchy, 98, 100, 151

personal discrimination. *See* gender discrimination; racial discrimination

positive attitude, 24

pregnancy, outside of marriage, 18

prejudice, universality of, 25

professional degrees of study participants. *See* study participants

professionals, Black: economic impact of segregation, 38; status, 35, 36

race: and gender, relationship between, 30; and social class, intersection of, 27. *See also* education; gender; gender discrimination; race relations; racial hierarchy; racial identity; racial pride

race relations, 147. *See also* racial discrimination; racial hierarchy; racial identity; racism

racial discrimination: confrontation of, 120; gender, relationship to (*see* gender discrimination); inevitability of, 12; laws addressing, 118, 119; post-1960s experiences, 115–118; in present society, 153–154; resistance to Black women's authority, 109, 116; salary, 104; self-employment situation, 107. *See also* race; race relations; racial hierarchy; racial identity; racism

racial hierarchy, 12, 14, 65

racial identity, 33; centrality of, 11–13; contradictions associated with, 12, 13; limits to opportunity, 12. *See also* racial pride

racial mixing, 45

racial pride, 13, 75–76, 156

racism, despite wealth, 12; institutional, 12; oppression, relationship between, 8; power, 12; self-protection from, 16; shielding children from, 14; systemic, 20; universality of, 25. *See also* racial discrimination; segregation

Reconstruction, 50

Reinharz, Shulamit, 163

religion. *See* church

requirements for study participants, 2. *See also* study participants

resistance, 168, 169; culture of, 93; economic, 38; ethos of sharing, 38; passive, 23; psychological, 24; taught by parents, 20; through positive attitude, 24. *See also* nonresistance

retirement, 8–9; caregiving to older relatives during, 137; church involvement during, 138–139; community involvement, 126, 138; family relationships following, 134, 135, 136–137; financial planning for, 130–131; "freedom," 124, 125; friendships, 133, 134; "giving back" to Black community, 140–147; health status of interviewees, 127-128; involvement with youth, 142, 143, 144, 145, 146; "joie de vivre" during, 158–159; life satisfaction, 125–127; loss of status, 149; meaningful activities, 131–132; preparations, 123; sharing experiences with younger generation, 123; sorority associations, 140; travel, 126, 135; "uplift" activities, 140–147; wisdom, 158

role models: Black, outside home, 70; in Black history, 76; in church, 51; study participants as, during retirement, 144. *See also* mentors
rural life, 34, 51, 68

salary discrimination. *See* gender discrimination; racial discrimination
sample size, 3
schools, 8; post-integration, 92. *See also* Black schools; education
segregation: career limitations, 90–91; church, relationship to, 55; in communities, 34–35; cruelties in working world, 102–103; economic issues for Blacks, 38; education under system, 8 (*see also* Black schools); effects on social contacts, 18–19, 46–47; ethos of sharing in Black community (*see* community life); on family, strains of, 30 (*see also* family); heterogeneity, 44; historical documentation, 8; inferiority of schools, 4, 91; on religious life, affect of, 49–50; self-containment, 34–35; shielding children from, 14; work as resistance during, 26; working in White world, 102–108. *See also* desegregation; racial discrimination; racism
self-confidence, 71; development of, 76–77; in intelligence, 76, 77, 78; shaped at church, 56; "specialness," 76, 77, 78–79. *See also* self-esteem
self-esteem, 24; as invisible armor, 26; positive despite segregation, 30. *See also* self-confidence
self-identity, positive, 14. *See also* self-esteem
self-reliance, 30
self-respect, 13
self-restraint, 57
sex discrimination. *See* gender discrimination
sexism. *See* gender discrimination
skin color differences: divisiveness of, 45; elitism, 63; and status, 45–46

slavery: church, role during, 50; ethos of sharing, 38; family lineage, 45; grandparent born into, 73; memories of elders, 13; racial mixing, 45
social categories, 7
social class. *See* class, social
sororities, 140
South (region), the, 36
status: homogenizations, 35; professionals, 35, 36; teachers, 35–36; women, 35, 36. *See also* skin color differences
Stoller, Eleanor, 7
strategizing, 22, 23
study: author backgrounds, 169–170; background, 161–162; collective biographies, 165–166; interview guidelines, 163–164; race and gender concerns of interviewers, 162–163; social class issues, 167–168; survival and resistance themes, 169–169. *See also* study participants
study participants: age, 3; careers, 88; class, social, 167–168; collective biographies, 165–166; education levels, 73; financial security, 128–131; friendships, 133; friendships, importance of, 155; geographical identity, 3–4, 15; health status, 127–128; how chosen, 2; marital status, 3; meaningful activities in retirement, 131–132, 133–140; as mentors in retirement, 143, 144; as models for positive retirement, 152, 157; as pioneers, 4; professional degrees, 3; religious profile, 49; requirements, 2; as role models, 144; sorority associations, 140
surrogate parenting, 70. *See also* community life; parenting
survival skills, 57

teaching, 88–89, 90, 93, 94, 95; desegregation experiences, 108; gender-based approaches, 95–96; holistic approach to, 96, 97;

teaching *(continued)*
teachers, respect for, 35–36, 92; teachers as motivators, 73; teachers' roles, 80, 81, 82, 83, 91–92; teacher status, 35–36; White colleagues, encounters with, 112, 113, 114; White parents' resentment, 110–111

"uplift work," 93, 98, 140, 141, 142, 157
urban life, 34, 51

virginity, 19
volunteerism, 131, 141
volunteerism by Black women, 33–34

Wade-Gayles, Gloria, 50
White Americans: Black Americans, avoidance issues for, 14–16; proximity to, 14, 15

White ancestry, 45. *See also* skin color differences
White privilege, 66–67
women in labor force, gender discrimination, 153. *See also* work
women's liberation movement, 115
work: blue collar, 103–104; dominant role, 26; expectation that children work, 27–28; holistic approach to helping racial family, 97; hostile environment, 120; importance for daughters, 29–30; integrated *vs.* segregated employment, 103; as resistance, 26. *See also* career; gender discrimination; work discrimination
work discrimination: federal government, 105, 106; geographic differences, 104–105; salary, 104, 106; self-employment situation, 107. *See also* gender discrimination

About the Authors

C. Ray Wingrove is a native Virginian who graduated from the University of Richmond with a B.A. in Sociology. He went on to earn his M.A. and Ph.D. from the University of North Carolina at Chapel Hill. He was an Assistant Professor of Sociology at the University of Georgia from 1964 until he assumed the position of Associate Professor of Sociology at the University of Richmond in 1971. At present, he is Professor of Sociology and holds the Irving May Chair in Human Relations at the University of Richmond. Much of his career has been devoted to the field of social gerontology. In recent years, much of his research has focused on older women.

Kathleen F. Slevin grew up in Northern Ireland. She attended University College, Dublin, for her undergraduate education. She came to the United States in 1971 and earned her M.A. and Ph.D. from the University of Georgia. Currently, she is Professor of Sociology and Chair of the Department of Sociology at the College of William and Mary in Virginia. In recent years, her research interests have focused on women in retirement.